High Spirits

High Spirits

H. PAUL JEFFERS

DRAWINGS BY KEVIN GORDON

LYONS & BURFORD, PUBLISHERS

Printed in the United States of America
Text design by Joel Friedlander Publishing Services, San Rafael, CA
10 9 8 7 6 5 4 3 2 1

Library of Congress Cataloging–in–Publication Data
Jeffers, H. Paul (Harry Paul), 1934–
        High spirits / H. Paul Jeffers.
             p. cm.
        Includes bibliographical references and index.
        ISBN 1–55821–553–0
        1. Liquors.   I. Title.
        TP597.J44   1997
        663'.5—dc21   97–8068
                                                                   CIP

For Jimmy Neary,
with fond memories of happy hours passed
in the grand pub that bears his name.

"As he brews, so shall he drink."

—BEN JONSON, 1598,
Everyman in His Humour

Contents

WHAT'LL YOU HAVE?

"And the men that were boys when I was a boy,
Shall sit and drink with me."

—HILAIRE BELLOC, 1870–1953

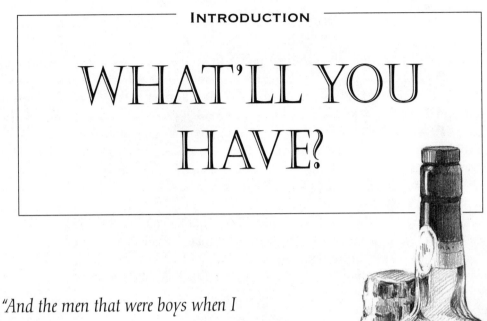

"Your tonic, *sahib.*"

Shaded by a huge blue-and-white striped lawn umbrella and shifting in a white rattan chair, I puffed on my pipe and wished the glass in the waiter's hand held a couple of fingers of Irish whiskey. But this was not the northwest frontier of the India of the British Empire and the poetry of Rudyard Kipling in the waning years of the nineteenth century. This was Peshawar in the modern state of Pakistan, and alcohol was not on Islam's approved list at Dean's Hotel, even if you did tote a U.S. passport.

"And here is your newspaper, *sahib,*" said the waiter, bowing and gently placing the *Frontier Post* on a round metal table while I wished he would quit calling me *sahib.* Besides making me feel even more alien, the word implied that I was some incarnation of Queen Victoria's imperialists who once had believed they would go on hustling the East forever. When I heard myself called *sahib* I wanted to shout that I was an American who not only believed in the struggle for freedom and democracy and self-determination just as ferociously as any Pakistani, Indian, or Afghani, but that I had devoted my life to the cause of liberty, which, all stripes of religious fundamentalism notwithstanding, included the right not to be denied a good stiff drink.

This attitude was due entirely to my ancestry—one fourth Welsh and three quarters Irish. Looking farther back, I'd run into Scots. This background makes me Celtic, a race that I am proud to note never ceased to struggle for their liberty even while *inventing* whiskey. The Gaelic term was *uisge beatha.* Pronounced "wheesa-bee," it soon became "whiskey" in English.

That it arrived in the United States was due mainly to the zeal of Irish and Scottish emigrants. Seeking political, religious, and economic liberties in the New World, they were unwilling to leave their unique libation behind. They rightly reasoned, "How sweet could liberty be without whiskey to drink to it?"

My libertarian views regarding imbibing hard liquor of all kinds are traceable to a descendant of those immigrants. My Uncle Harry Singleton was a pug-nosed Irishman known as Toots, who in my boyhood was the proprietor of a little watering hole called—what else?—Toots' Bar. On a corner in Norristown, Pennsylvania, it was the first such place I ever set my foot in. Because of my tender years I was allowed to drink only ginger ale. Education in the hard stuff had to wait until my college years, and then not before I had reached my twenty-first birthday, the legal age for drinking in the Keystone State in the 1950s.

I am proud to note that in ordering my first drink in a bar in Philadelphia, I did not duplicate the faux pas of young Holden Caulfield in J. D. Salinger's *Catcher in the Rye* of asking for "a scotch and bourbon." With the bold assurance of youth, I demanded Old Bushmills on the rocks. (I had learned from Uncle Harry that it was Irish whiskey.) However, before it was set down in front of me on a long, gleaming bar around the corner from the Reading Terminal I had to endure a skeptical bartender demanding my I.D.

Since that historic afternoon in that dim establishment off Market Street in the City of Brotherly Love, I have nursed Irish in many manly tumblers. And scotch, of course. Rum and Coca-Cola in sophisticated highball glasses. Dry martinis in long-stemmed chalices that I had been told were modeled on the shape of a young woman's breast. I savored Manhattans in Manhattan. Old Fashioneds at the now gone and sorely missed Astor Bar in Times Square. Creamy brandy Alexanders at the Waldorf. I drank Mexican tequila from vessels with salt-encrusted rims in a saloon across the street from the Alamo in Antonio, vodka in cities that offered quiet bistros ideal for carrying out a little Cold War espionage, cognac in a French restaurant with anti-hand grenade screens on its windows in Saigon, and sake in exotic locales of the Orient that would do James Bond proud. There was the ouzo of Greece in a taverna in Athens while admiring the moonlight on the ruins of the Parthenon. In Belfast, Northern Ireland, it was Old Bushmills. Jimmy Neary's Irish mecca in New York sold me Jamesons from the Irish Republic. I sipped fine English gins and tonic at the Sherlock Holmes Pub in London. And each year I invited some friends to share the contents of my liquor cabinet at a party on Sherlock's birthday (January 6). After a pilgrimage to 221-B Baker Street in 1982 I had a glorious twelve-year-old single-malt scotch while sailing home aboard the QE2. In the bar car of the storied Orient Express it was Napoleon brandy. And at Harry's Bar in Venice, nursing bourbon neat, I imagined I was Ernest Hemingway awaiting the arrival of Ava Gardner.

There were beers and wines, as well, but this is a book about what Uncle Harry called "the real stuff," for in Toots' Bar there was far more drinking of whiskey than anything else.

In *High Spirits* I offer a comprehensive book on the world of the "hard" alcoholic beverages—scotches, Irish, bourbons, and blended whiskey; brandy; gin; vodka; rum; tequila; and liqueurs. Beginning with the development of spirits in the Old World and New, it is a practical how-to guide, as well as a comprehensive and, I hope, entertaining look at social, political, and cultural aspects of drinking in the United States; women and drinking; the use of alcohol as depicted in the arts and literature; famous and infamous personalities who imbibed "strong drink"; pitfalls of abuse and alcoholism; and the status of quality spirits in the United States and around the world. Plus some delightfully quotable and spirited words on the topic, including toasts.

As you settle down to read with drink at hand, I offer you my favorite: "Let your boat of life be light, packed with only what you need—a homely home, and simple pleasures, one or two friends worth the name, someone to love you, and a cigar or pipe or two, enough to eat and enough to wear, and a little more than enough to drink; because thirst is a dangerous thing."

PART I

WATER OF LIFE—
THE WHISKEYS

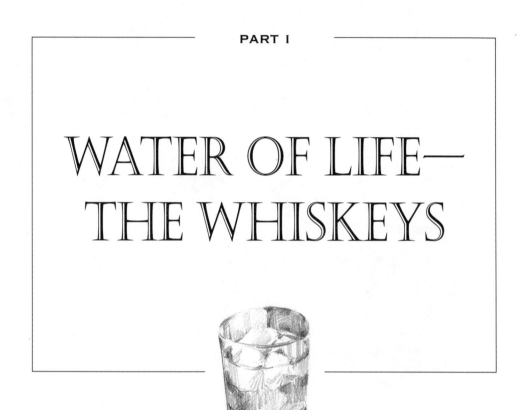

1

SOVEREIGN LIQUOR

"If all be true that I do think,
There are five reasons we should drink:
Good wine—a friend—or being dry—
Or lest we should be by and by—
Or any other reason why."

—HENRY ALDRICH, 1647–1710
Five Reasons for Drinking

Whether standing with a glass in your hand amidst strangers at a bar or sharing libations with friends at home, you can start a pretty good argument about whether humanity is the result of an act of God, as told in the Book of Genesis, or the combination of science's Big Bang theory and Darwin's thesis that mankind is the evolutionary proof of the survival of the fittest. But there is one point that can't be debated: There is no life without water.

If you believe the Bible, the first people to drink it were Adam and Eve. If you follow science and Darwin, they were apelike predecessors of ourselves in a very distant age, probably scratching out an existence somewhere on land we call Africa. Whoever they were, they and their descendants survived on water for ages. But somewhere along the way, one of them—a very clever, possibly quite brilliant, but certainly very bored individual—decided to spice up the taste of the stuff with a bit of flavoring, probably by squeezing into the water the juice of whatever fruit or grain happened to be handy. Maybe it was accidental. The event happened before the advent of writing, so history stands mute on the subject. Nor does it record exactly how someone figured out that if the added ingredient remained in the water and fermented for a while, it lent a very pleasant kick to the drinking of it. All we know from the written record of humankind's rise in the Judeo-Christian–Muslim holy books is that thousands of years ago, lowly water found a competitor in wine.

Hand in hand with the fledgling wine industry came those who saw the potential for mischief in consuming too much alcohol. The Prophet Isaiah warned, "Woe unto them that rise up early in the morning, that they may follow strong drink" (Isaiah 5:11).

We also know from other chronicles and memoirs of ancient peoples that somebody outside of the Holy Land had discovered how to make strong drink. In 23 B.C., Horace of Greece wrote in *Odes*, "Now is the time for drinking, now the time to beat the earth with unfettered foot." Both Greeks and Romans, as well as other peoples in the ancient world, had at least one god of drinking.

The Egyptians were expert at making beer. Indeed, in 1996, when long-dried-out traces of the Egyptian variety—dating back at least five thousand years—were analyzed, the stuff was reproduced and put on sale commercially at a price even King Tut would gasp at.

While wine was probably the earliest replacement for water, with beer coming in second as an alternative way to quench one's thirst, who invented each has not been recorded.

But we do know it was somebody in Ireland who concocted a means of converting grain to the *uisge beatha* that became whiskey.

Irish and Scotch

The first written mention of whiskey in Ireland dates to the fifteenth century.

Few and far between could a wanderer in Erin find a little thatch-roofed house that did not have a still in which to mingle the three essential elements of whiskey: water, earth, and fire. The former abounded fresh and clear in Ireland's countless lakes, brooks, and streams. From the earth came grain and yeast, as well as an apparently endless supply of bogs from which to dig peat to fuel the fire.

While the Irish in their wee cottages with their outdoor stills called their new drink "water of life," it was not made for the medicinal benefits discovered in it by an Irish physician of the seventeenth century. He wrote: "It scowereth all scurf; it sloweth age; it cutteth flegme; it pounceth the stone; it expelleth gravel; it keepeth the head from whirling, the mouth from maffling, the stomach from wambling, the heart from swelling, the belly from wirtching, the guttes from rumbling . . . it is a sovereign liquor."

Around the same time, Sir Walter Raleigh—who also grasped the virtues of tobacco—noted that during a visit to Ireland, a friend who lived in Cork had given him a "supreme present" in the form of a thirty-two-gallon keg of whiskey. As he had done with tobacco, he lost no time in introducing the delightful drink to the court of Queen Elizabeth I.

But it was the successor to Good Queen Bess who envisioned in whiskey the possibility of a thriving and enticingly taxable business enterprise. Although King James I proved to be no friend of tobacco, denouncing it as a "stinking weed" and all but outlawing it, he appointed Sir Thomas Phillips as his deputy in the Irish province of Ulster and bestowed upon him the authority to grant licenses to whiskey distillers. That James, who had been king of Scotland before he assumed the throne of England, sent Phillips to Ireland is evidence that whiskey had not yet made its debut in James's homeland.

No slouch at lining his own pockets, Phillips built his own distillery on the banks of the Bush River in County Antrim, and named both it and its product "Bushmills." Presently, the roll of Irish whiskey makers came to include John Jameson, who opened his distillery in Dublin in 1780. Eleven years later, John Power also set up there. In 1825 it was the Murphy brothers who built a distillery at Midleton, near Cork. It boasted the world's largest pot still. Holding three thousand gallons, it was in service for 150 years.

As to the second people of the British Isles to produce the nectar of distilled grain, for evidence that the folk of Scotland took to spirits one need turn only to the work of their greatest poet, Robert Burns. Who has not, whether with a glass of wine, beer, whiskey, or some other potent potion, welcomed a new year by singing Bobby's sentimental salute to past and future?

> *For auld lange syne, my dear,*
> *For auld lange syne.*
> *We'll take a cup o' kindness yet*
> *For auld lange syne.*

Making whiskey rather than wine in Ireland and Scotland was due to climate. Cold and soggy, the lands of the Celts were not hospitable to the delicate nature of grape vines. But Ireland and Scotland were fine for growing the chief ingredient of scotch and Irish whiskeys—barley.

An annual cereal plant (member of the grass family), it is first turned into malt.

In Ireland, unlike in Scotland, malted barley is dried in closed ovens rather than over peat fires, thus the smokier taste in scotch whiskey.
Courtesy Irish Distillers Limited

Making Malt

When barley is steeped in water, the heart of the grain (the embryo) germinates and secretes an enzyme (diastase). This material converts grain starches to sugars (saccharification). The resulting soupy mixture, called green malt, is removed from the germination container and is spread out to a depth of about a foot for a period of up to two weeks for drying and cooling (curing). In the era before mechanization, this required manually turning the mash to dissipate built-up heat. Today, curing is done in slowly rotating drums (kilns). Many of today's big whiskey distillers reduce production costs by turning for supplies to outside specialists known as maltsters.

A difference between Irish and scotch is in the source of grain for malting. Scotch is made entirely from malted barley. Irish is made from a blend of malted and unmalted barley, with oats, rye, and wheat added to the blend.

Another difference is in the method of heating during the malting. Scotch malt is made over peat fires that give scotch its distinctive smoky flavor. Irish is also heated over peat, but in closed kilns. It gets its flavoring through blending.

With the drying completed, the malt resembles crisp toast and contains extraneous material that must be removed before the malt can be milled and readied for the next step on the road to becoming whiskey.

MASHING

After sifting out (dressing) impurities, such as chaff and rootlets, the malt is coarsely milled and mixed with hot water in a huge vat (mash tun). In the resulting gloppy porridge (wort), the diastase springs into action to convert any remaining starch into fermentable sugars. This mixture is strained and drained through the bottom of the mash tun into a container. In the exquisitely direct language of whiskey-making, this apparatus under and at the back of the tun is called a receiver/underback.

These drainings are known as distiller's beer, wort, setback, back, or mash. To be sure everything is collected in the tun, a second mashing is done with even hotter water.

This is followed by a final flushing of the tun with less water. Most of the resulting mash is pumped out and added to the next supply of malt. The purpose is to engender a consistency of flavor between batches.

What's left in the tun (draff or grains) is removed and sold as animal feed.

Whether the first two collections are called wort, back, or mash, they are ready for the next stage: the production of alcohol that in time will evolve into whiskey.

FERMENTATION

After cooling, the mash is loaded into fermentation vats (wash backs) and yeast is added. As in making bread and beer, the yeast releases enzymes that work on the mash to convert maltose into alcohol and carbon dioxide gas. After thirty-six to forty hours of fermenting and frequent stirring, the liquid (wash) is drained into a wash receiver. The whole process is called "brewing," but it is now that the process of making whiskey departs from the means of making beer.

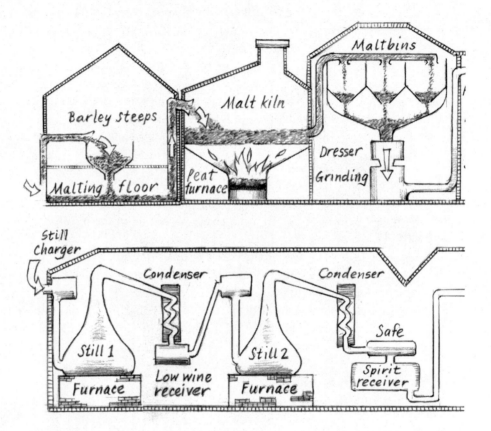

The anatomy of a distillery.

Map by Kevin Gordon

DISTILLATION

Distillation is the boiling of fermented liquor in a closed container and condensing the steam. The basis of making whiskey and other distilled drinks is that alcohol boils at a lower temperature than water. By boiling the fermented grain in a closed container with a long spout or tubing, the alcohol may be cooled, condensed, and collected. For scotch whiskey, the distilling is done twice. Irish is distilled three times. The apparatus used in both is a still. There are two varieties: pot and patent.

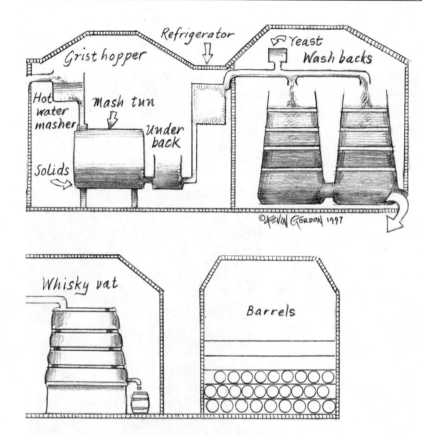

©KEVIN GORDON 1997

Pot Stills

A pot still—an immense onion-shaped, copper-lined container with a long, narrow neck and condensing tubes (coil or worm)—is quite literally a pot for boiling. Initially, a pot still produces an extremely strong liquid called low wine, which is distilled again in an adjoining, smaller spirit-still. As this liquid is flowing, it passes through a spirit safe— a window that allows the whiskey to be examined visually or drawn off for testing—employed as a means of quality control by a stillman. Although the liquid is far too hot to be handled, the stillman can check it both visually and with instruments for cloudiness: After the addition of a drop of distilled water, the alcohol should remain clear. The stillman also uses instruments to test for specific gravity and proof.

Proof is a measurement of alcohol content by percentage. An early means to test for the strength of the alcohol was to add some gunpowder to a mixture of the alcohol and water, and put a flame to it. If the damp gunpowder ignited, the alcohol "proved." Today's distillers determine that a customer will get a suitable bang for his buck by testing for proof with a hydrometer.

Known as new whiskey, the distillate emerges in declining proof and purity. The first part (foreshot) is much too potent and impure, although it does contribute to the flavoring of the whiskey that the stillman determines to be potable (high wines). This is known as the middle cut.

The remainder (feint) is weak and is saved for redistilling in the next batch. What's left of the feint after a second distillation (spent lees) is watery and is discarded. The output of a still is known as a batch.

MATURATION

Whiskey is aged to tone down the toxicity and harshness, and to give it a smoother taste. The product that the stillman's knowing eye judges fit to become whiskey begins the maturing process in oak casks of varying sizes, depending on the requirements set out by the distiller. A butt will hold upward of 108 gallons; a puncheon ranges between 90 and 120; hogsheads hold 54; American barrels, 40 gallons.

The traditionally preferred cask for maturing malt whiskey in Scotland was one that had previously been used in the mak-

Pot still of the Stitzler-Weller Distillery in 1960. Known as a doubler, it distilled the alcohol twice to raise proof and ensure a smooth drink.
Courtesy United Distillers Archive, Stitzler-Weller Collection, W. L. Weller and Sons files

POT STILL
DOUBLER Nº 1
CAP. 3,000 GALS.

Heaven Hill distillery worker Tommy Green checking the proof of whiskey in a holding tank as it flows out of the still.
Courtesy Heaven Hill

ing of sherry wine. This choice was largely based on the fact that the barrels were inexpensive. Eventually, because gin and whiskey replaced sherry as the preferred before-dinner drink, the sherry casks became too hard to get, requiring pennywise Scottish distillers to turn elsewhere for barrels, including to America for secondhands from bourbon makers.

How long any whiskey matures in wood depends on the country of origin, pertinent laws, and the intent of the distiller. Aging of particular brands will be discussed in subsequent chapters.

During the aging, some of the contents of the casks evaporate. The loss amounts to about 2 percent a year. That is about forty-five liters of pure spirit over a decade. Distillers call the lost vapors "the angels' share."

Patent Stills

Invented by Robert Stein, a distiller in Kilbagie, Clackmannan, Scotland, in 1826, and improved in 1830 by Aeneas Coffey, a tax official in Dublin, the patent still differs from the pot still in design and operation. While pot distilling is a labor-intensive process and requires shutting production from time to time for emptying and cleaning, the patent still incorporates the advantages of the mid-nineteenth century's industrial revolution by introducing mechanization. Consisting of a pair of columns standing seventy feet high,

All Irish whiskey must be matured in oak casks for a minimum of three years.
Courtesy Irish Distillers Limited

this continuous still receives cold fermented wort and lets it trickle over a series of plates that deliver steam. It was a precursor of production-line systems that became the basis of manufacturing automobiles and, as fans of Lucille Balls's television series *I Love Lucy* will recall, candy-making factories.

Introduction of the patent still facilitated the rise and availability, as well as popularity, of blended grain whiskeys.

But it was the pot still that traveled across the Atlantic Ocean and made what would become the United States of America a whiskey-drinking country. It also presented the first test of the new nation's fragile experiment in a unique way of government.

The American Way

The first still was brought to America in the sixteenth century by the Spanish. But it was used to distill the Mexican agave plant to make a precursor of tequila.

English settlers preferred rum, and by the middle of the seventeenth century were making it in Massachusetts from molasses that came up from the Caribbean Islands in one leg of a triangle in trade that sent the New England rum to Africa for slaves, who were sold in the Caribbean for sugarcane and molasses. Rum continued as the main alcoholic drink of Britain's American colonists right up to the War of Independence. It was rum that was hoisted in Fraunce's Tavern in New York for George Washington's farewell to the army.

Washington soon gave up civilian life at his home in Virginia to return to New York to take the oath of office as president of the United States in 1789. The very next year, he faced a domestic crisis that challenged not only his presidential authority as commander in chief of the army but the future of the brand–new democracy, all because of a tax on American whiskey that excited its Scottish and Irish distillers to take up weapons against the tax collectors.

Because of religious and political repressions imposed by England, these Celtic immigrants had left home for the British colonies in America in the early eighteenth century. Having settled in western Pennsylvania, they wasted no time in building stills to convert corn, rye, and barley into whiskey. The brew became their primary medium of exchange. Suddenly, they were shocked to discover that their newly created government had enacted the Excise Tax on Spiritous Liquors. It demanded they fork over a portion of the proceeds of their stills. Many of them being veterans of the war that had been fought over taxation, they resented the intrusion of the new government into their lives, not to mention objecting to sharing their livelihood with the government.

History records the manifestation of their resentment as the Whiskey Rebellion. Rather than pay the tax, the whiskey makers raised a ragtag army to resist any attempts by the government to enforce the law.

Although President Washington feared that the army might not follow orders to march against fellow Americans, the distillers discovered that Washington's anxiety had been groundless. With no shots fired, the uprising evaporated as quickly as the steam from stills.

RYE WHISKEY

I'll go to the holler
And build me a still;
I'll give you a gallon
For a five-dollar bill.
Chorus:
Rye whiskey, rye whiskey, I cry;
If I don't get rye whiskey
I surely will die.
Way up on Clinch mountain
I wander alone;
I'm drunk as a devil,
Just leave me alone.
Chorus.
I'll eat when I'm hungry,
I'll drink when I'm dry,
If a tree don't fall on me,
I'll live till I die.
—American folksong

17

The White Rabbit saloon, opened by Jack Daniel in Lynchburg, Tennessee, when he found it difficult to send out whiskey he made. Marketing problems disappeared with the coming of the railroad.
Courtesy Jack Daniel Distillery

Defeated but undaunted, the rebels promptly packed up all their possessions, and their stills, and headed farther west to a spot renowned for its good water and fine grain–growing land that was a more comfortable distance from revenue agents. The place some chose to settle was Kentucky, while others trekked onward to Tennessee. The whiskey was distilled from corn, barley, and rye. Offering drinkers an assertive flavor, Kentucky's whiskey is bourbon (named for Bourbon County) and Tennessee's is Tennessee. They have also been widely referred to as sour mash whiskey. Both are categorized along with Canadian whiskeys as "American."

Whatever their name, the drinking of them fueled American spirits in steadily growing numbers for the next 178 years. Then doughboys who had marched off to win the War to End All Wars, to the cadences of Irving Berlin's "Over There," carried home with them a taste for a whiskey that had not been widely available nor very popular in the United States prior to 1918. As they trooped home to the tune of "How you gonna keep them down on the farm after they've seen Paree?" they were also singing praises to scotch.

In the United States before the war, Irish had been the choice in imported whiskeys. However, with the outbreak of hostilities, the neutral Irish government restricted its export.

PROOF

Alcoholic content is designated in degrees and called proof. It is calculated with a hydrometer in which distillate is heated and weighed in comparison to an equal amount of distilled water at the same temperature.
In British distilling, alcohol at fifty-one degrees Fahrenheit is twelve-thirteenths the weight of water.
One-hundred proof on the British scale is 114.2 percent by the American method of measurement, or 14.2 percent "over proof." A hundred proof on the American scale is 87.7 British.
When an American whiskey's label states "80 proof," contents of the bottle are actually 40 percent alcohol. The rest is water.

This required thirsty American warriors who didn't take well to English gin and warm beer to look elsewhere for their sustenance from the water of life. To their lasting delight they discovered the whiskey of Scotland and wanted it when they reached home.

Even as the men of the American Expeditionary Force sailed back from Europe with a zest for scotch, they and the descendants of the veterans of the Whiskey Rebellion felt the heavy hand of government in the form of the 1919 Volstead Act. It ushered in fourteen years of the most disastrous social experiment in U.S. history. Suddenly, Prohibition made it impossible to get a good stiff drink of any sort legally.

Among the results of the closing of legal distilleries were not only the rise of organized criminal gangs eager to quench a thirst for drink in the form of bootleg booze, but the ruin of domestic whiskey makers. Officially going dry sparked interest in illicit scotch, Irish, and other foreign-made liquors, as well as a zest for gin, so easily made that you could concoct it in your bathtub.

So widespread was illicit distillation that between 1919 and 1929 the output of corn sugar by American farmers increased six-fold. By the end of that decade, eight times as much liquor was being turned out by illicit stills in the United States as all the liquor being smuggled into the country by bootleggers.

In his informal history of the 1920s, *Only Yesterday*, Frederick Lewis Allen wrote that this "overwhelming flood

A Prohibition-time raid results in the confiscation of distillation equipment.
Courtesy New York Public Library

of outlaw liquor" introduced into the American scene the indelible image of Prohibition as fourteen years of hip flasks uplifted above faces both masculine and feminine at big football games; the speakeasy; gangster bootleggers; "well–born damsels with one foot on a brass rail, tossing off Martinis"; federal atttorneys padlocking nightclubs; the Prohibition agents Izzy Einstein and Moe Smith "putting on a series of comic–opera disguises" to capture bootleggers; and revenue agents mistaking a Canadian ship named *I'm Alone* for a rum–runner and sinking it on the high seas, much to the dismay of the Canadian government.

Prohibition also saw in neighboring Canada in 1928 the opening of Distillers Corporation–Seagram Ltd. Founded by Samuel Bronfman, the new distilling enterprise offered a mature, high–quality blended drink. With warehouses bulging with inventory as Repeal took effect in December 1933, Seagram added a new category to the roster of North American whiskey: Canadian.

Following Prohibition, all domestic distillers experienced a period of prosperity that encompassed the Depression, World War II, and three decades of the Cold War. But in the 1970s a coming–of–age postwar generation known as the baby boomers became health-conscious. Thinking they could live forever if they simply "cut out" something, they began eschewing any product that appeared to impinge on prospects for endless life. As tobacco and red–meat consumption suffered from these anxieties, so did whiskey. White wine was "in." Scotch, Irish, bourbons, blends, and even martinis were out. Imported mineral waters became the vogue. It seemed that everyone was quaffing Perrier water.

As an example, a friend of the author of this book who for ten years drank scotch at my annual Sherlock Holmes birthday party suddenly switched to ginger ale! Other guests who used to finish off many bottles of my best liquor left them untouched in favor of "softer" drinks. My finest scotch, Irish, bourbons, gin, vodka, rum, and tequila went begging and back onto the shelves of my liquor cabinet.

But good whiskey never goes bad, and popular tastes change. Presently, sons and daughters of the boomers reached the drinking age. What had been out of favor came back into style. Children of non– and anti–smoking parents were lighting up premium cigars in bars. After a sales decline of 30 to 35 percent in the 1980s, sales of liquor rebounded.

The *New York Daily News* noted on May 28, 1996: "Our Spirits Are Soaring."

The article took note that those who were choosing to drink liquor differed from their imbibing predecessors. These people were knowledgeable and savvy about whiskey and other spirits. They did not want to step up to a bar and order a scotch or a bourbon. They needed to ask for a particular *brand*.

Had they taken a cue from Edward FitzGerald's *The Rubaiyat of Omar Khayyam?* "Drink," the poem declared, "for once dead, you never shall return."

They certainly appeared to have taken a lead from Oscar Wilde. A hundred years ago he quipped, "I have made an important discovery. Alcohol, if taken in sufficient quantities, produces all the effects of intoxication."

Perhaps they had discovered wisdom in a rhyme of Scotland's poet laureate, Bobby Burns:

> *Inspiring bold John Barleycorn!*
> *What dangers thou can make us scorn!*
> *Wi' tippenny, we fear nae evil;*
> *Wi' usquebae we'll face the devil!*

2

SCOTCH

"From the bonny bells of heather

They brewed a drink long-syne,

Was sweeter far than honey.

Was stronger far than wine."

—ROBERT LOUIS STEVENSON, 1850–94

More than a century after the death of the Scot who delighted children with *Treasure Island* and terrified adults with *Dr. Jekyll and Mr. Hyde*, the whiskey of Scotland that Stevenson had extolled in such poetic terms suddenly appeared to be rivaling Scotland's national game (golf) in the hearts of Americans. At a time when spirits were suffering a decline in consumption in the United States, scotch—especially single-malt—enjoyed a growth in demand at bars and in liquor stores. Scotch "tastings" became available for novices and those who were simply curious as to what was behind all the fuss over a whiskey that had been around for more than four centuries.

Quick to offer explanations for the phenomenon, sociologists and analysts of popular culture noted that the fervor for scotch was most evident in the males of the post–World War II baby boom generation who in the 1990s found themselves middle-aged, rebelling against the increasing restrictions of a "politically correct" era, and prosperous enough to afford the indulgence of a need for self-assertiveness. These included driving prestigious cars, collecting expensive jewelry to accent a designer wardrobe, acquisition of electronic gadgets of all kinds, taking exotic vacations, and living in a luxurious home with a fine wine cellar stocked with just the right vintage for each course of a gourmet dinner that would be followed by old cognac and a premium cigar.

With a variety of whiskeys available, what was there about scotch that elevated it to the preferred status it came to hold?

Author Michael Beazley in his handy pocket guide to whiskey described it as "an elemental elixir" available in such a wide range of aromas and flavors that the drink provides an "inexhaustible opportunity to explore and experiment, to taste and enjoy."

Master of Malt John Lamond wrote in *The Malt Whiskey File* that scotch is a distillation of the colors, flavor, and atmosphere of Scotland in which "soft air, water, agriculture, and traditional craftsmanship combine to produce the world's premier spirit."

The Classic Malts of Scotland Society claims that the drinking of scotch whiskeys is a journey of discovery, not just of the whiskeys, but of the land of their origin.

A country described as a lumpy mass of land that juts out of the northernmost part of Britain, Scotland is a jagged hunk sliced and spliced by lakes, inlets, bays, firths, rivers, and streams. In terms of whiskey, Scotland is divided into distinctive regions, each with a whiskey of singular character.

Highlands (northern and western) are hilly and rocky with windswept moors. They are separated from flat, wet Lowlands to the south by the Highland Line: Drawn on a map in 1784 by a tax collector (who else?), this arbitrary bisection extends from Glasgow to Dundee. Everything to the north is Highlands. The key water feature is the River Spey. Flowing southwest to northeast, it is fed by numerous tributaries that carry pure waters from springs and lochs of another geological feature, the Grampian Mountains. North of this range lie the Lowlands of the Highlands, not to be confused with the Lowlands to the south. With soil so prime that it is known as the Garden of Scotland, the Lowlands of the Higlands are also rich in peat.

Coastal plains of the West Highlands are a source of barley and the location of one of Scotland's oldest distilleries, at Oban.

The regions of Scotland.
Map by Kevin Gordon

Speyside is the valley of the second-longest but swiftest-running river in the British Isles, in which the majority of the distilleries are found. But before the whiskey trade became a legal enterprise in Scotland, those who were to turn into legitimate distillers had been engaged in a brisk and profitable trade in the illicit making and smuggling of it. So superb were these swashbuckling, freebooting Speysiders at their work that in 1822 the Duke of Gordon told members of the House of Lords in London that the Highlanders were "born distillers." Speyside malts are generally sweet with a light body.

A smaller tributary of the Spey is the Livet. The original whiskey of the region was called a Glenlivet. The first Livet distiller was George Smith, licensed in 1823 on recommendation of the Duke of Richmond and Gordon. Any other product adopting the name Glenlivet must by law prefix another name. For example, the distillery founded in 1840 by the brothers John and James Grant is labeled Glen Grant–Glenlivet.

Also known as the Glen whiskeys, Glenlivets will have a deep mellowness and ripe fullness, along with a delicacy of aroma and rather subtle peatiness.

The Lowlands. In 1787, Robert Burns called the region of the Lowlands known as East Lothian "the most glorious corn country I have ever seen." Surrounding the Scottish capital of

---

A SCOTCH BRAND PRONUNCIATION GUIDE*

Aberlour	Aber-lower	Glenglassaugh	Glen Glass-och
Allt-a-Bhainne	Oly-a-vane	Glen Mhor	Glen Moar
Auchentoshan	Oshen-toe-shen	Glenmorangie	Glen Mran-jee
Auchroisk	Oth-rusk	Glentauchers	Glen-tockers
Balmenach	Bal-may-nock	Glenury	Glen-yoo-ree
Bruichladdich	Brew-ich-laddie	Islay	Eye-la
Bunnahabhain	Boon-a-havun	Knockando	Nock-an-doo
Caol Ila	Kall-eea	Laphroaig	La-froyg
Cardhu	Kar-doo	Magdalene	Mag-da-leen
Clynelish	Kline-leesh	Pittyvaich	Pitt-ee-vay-ich
Craigellachie	Krai-gell-ah-chee	Pulteney	Pult-nay
Dailuaine	Dall-yew-an	Strathisla	Strath-eye-la
Dallas Dhu	Dallas Doo	Tamdhu	Tam-DOO
Drumguish	Droo-oo-ish	Tamnavulin	Tem-VOO-lin
Edradour	Edra-dower	Tomintoul	Tom-in-towel
Glen Garioch	Glen-gee-ree	Tullibardine	Tully-bard-eye-en

*If you fail to find your favorite scotch here, take no offense. I have included only distillery names that are difficult to pronounce.

Edinburgh, the red earth has provided its farmers a prosperous living and given the area the title the Larder of Edinburgh. Its sunny and dry climate produces some of the best brewing and distilling barley in Europe. These distilleries offer a variety of mild malts that deliver a dram of light and smooth-spirited drink.

The Western Islands. These are the numerous chunks of land known as the Hebrides. They include Jura, the Mull of Kintyre (home of Campbeltown malts), Orkney, and the Isle of Skye. They distill whiskeys more notable than any for being smoky in aroma and taste.

Islay. Also one of the Hebrides Islands and pronounced "eye-lah," it is called Lord of the Isles. It is the home of the Lagavulin Distillery and five others. Islays are the most heavily peated, pungent, and weightiest of scotch malts.

Reviewing the significance of geography to malt whiskey, Michael Brander wrote in his guide to scotch that "the products of the individual distilleries remain each as different from the next as claret from burgundy or sherry from port. It is this that makes the malt whiskies so satisfying to savour even if there may be general similarities of type amongst the various groups."

The Basics of Malt Whiskeys

Malt whiskey is the product of the pot-still method.

While there are pot stills in Ireland, and even in Japan, genuine scotch is made only in Scotland, where there are more than one hundred malt-whiskey distillers.

Under terms of the laws of Scotland, no scotch may be sold that is under three years of age. Most are twelve years old or older. It does not age further after bottling. That is why bottle labels generally don't state the year of bottling, only the number of years the whiskey spent aging in oak casks.

Single-malt scotch-whiskey bottle labels will state "Product of Scotland," that it is a pure malt whiskey, the area where it was made, the name of the distillery, the alcohol content (proof or volume by percent), and the quantity in the bottle, measured in milliliters (ml).

If it is a mixture of malts (blended) the label will state that the contents are a product of Scotland and that they have been distilled, blended, and bottled in Scotland. The age refers to how long the youngest of ingredients spent aging in oak.

A scotch's age is defined by the number of years it spends in casks. Once bottled it does not age further.
Courtesy New York Public Library

COLOR

Directly out of a still, whiskey is virtually colorless—only a very light straw tint may sometimes be visible. The color of the finished product is fostered by the age and history of the oak barrels employed in the aging process. The spectrum runs from clear to dark. Coloring may also be produced by adding caramel or sherry.

AROMA AND TASTE

"What does scotch taste like?"

The question was posed in the play and movie *Mr. Roberts* to the title character. Doug Roberts was a lieutenant in the U.S. Navy serving as executive officer of a supply ship in the Pacific who longed for duty on a destroyer before the war ended. With a frown, Roberts replied to the doctor that scotch always reminded him of iodine.

The issue of taste was vital because the two men were making phony scotch for young Ensign Frank Pulver. He had promised a curvaceous navy nurse that were she to visit his quarters aboard ship, he would share a bottle of scotch with her. Because he had no such thing, an ersatz product was created by the doctor from medicinal alcohol, half a bottle of Coca-Cola for coloring, and iodine for taste. To "age the hell out of it," the doc added a drop of hair oil with a coal-tar base.

After a sip, Roberts declared, "You know, Doc, that does taste like scotch!"

Actually, a good scotch should have the taste and aroma of peat. As in wine, the smell of whiskey is called nose. Unlike in wines and brandies, the fragrance of whiskey is not enhanced by a swirling of the glass holding it. Nor is the taste made any more vivid by swishing it around within the mouth.

As in the vocabulary of wine tasting, a drink of whiskey is described in nouns: color, nose, mouth (taste), body, fullness, depth, and finish (aftertaste). There are colorful adjectives by which to define the experience: smoky, peaty, silky, rich, velvety, smooth, and mature.

When imbibed it should feel smooth and without a sense of harsh burning in mouth and throat. It shouldn't be bitter, but it may have a slightly medicinal taste. As with cigars, the taste is affected by the circumstances surrounding the experience. The consensus of connoisseurs is that scotch is not at its best if it is chilled with ice, as in "on the rocks." Among the knowledgeable, the very idea of mixing fine scotch with something brings shudders of disdain. Yet there are many ways to do so, from Rob Roy to old-fashioned to whiskey sour. (Recipes may be found in Part III, Mixology.)

Choices are enormous. One collector of single-malt scotches has a trove of more than four hundred. An easy way of comparing the malts from all the regions is to taste an assortment imported to the United States by Schieffelin & Somerset Co., New York, as "Classic Malts of Scotland":

Name, Age	Region
Craggamore, 12	Speyside
Dalwhinnie, 15	Central Highlands
Oban, 14	Western Higlands
Glenkinchie, 10	Lowlands
Talisker, 10	Isle of Skye
Lagavulin, 16	Islay

Just as you can get into argument over Adam and Eve versus Big Bang and Darwin, judgments on the quality of whiskey brands will vary from person to person. The opinions of this author are on the basis of personal experience, a consensus of knowing friends and bartenders, as well as views of professional tasters. They are here in alphabetical order with age and strength, or alcohol by volume. *NA* means no age is listed on the label. Some are listed by the year in which they were distilled or bottled. *Cask strength* means straight-out-of-barrel strength. Regions of origin are indicated Highland (H), Speyside (S), Lowland (L), and islands by name. Body is rated light (L), medium (M), and full (F). They are rated superior (S), excellent (E), good (G), and fair.

Name/Age/Strength	Region	Body/Rating	
Aberfeldy	H	M	G
10/40			
15/43			
Aberlour	S	M–F	E
10/40			
NA/100			
1970			
NA/43			
Antique			
Allt-a-Bhainne	S	L	G
13/43			
Ardbeg	Islay	M–F	E
10/40			
18/43			
Ardmore	S	L	G
12/56.2			
Auchentoshan	L	L	G
NA/40			
10/40			
21/43			
Auchroisk	S	M	G
10/43			
Aultmore	S	M–F	G
12/40			
12/43			
13/46			
Balblair	H	L	G
5/40			
10/40			

Name/Age/Strength	Region	Body/Rating	
1964/40			
1957/40			
Balmenach	S	M–F	G
12/43			
The Balvenie	S	M–F	E
10/40			
The Balvenie Double Wood			
12/43			
The Balvenie Single Barrel			
15/50.4			
The Balvenie Founder's Reserve			
10/43			
Banff Connoisseurs Choice	S	M	G
1947/40			
Ben Nevis	H	F	E
15/60.9			
26/59			
1972/55.6			
Benriach	S	L	E
10/43			
Benrinnes	S	M–F	E
15/43			
Cadenhead's, 19/50.2			
Connoisseurs 1969/40			
Benromach	S	M–F	E
1971/40			
Bladnoch	L	L	E
8/40			
10/40			
1984/40			
28/42.5			
Blair Athol	H	M	G
8/40			
12/43			
Bowmore	Islay	L–M	E
10/40			

Body: light (L), medium (M), full (F).   Regions: Highland (H), Speyside (S), Lowland (L).   Overall: superior (S), excellent (E), good (G), fair.

Name/Age/Strength	Region	Body/Rating	
12/43			
NA/43			
21/43			
25/43			
29/49.4			
30/50			
Bowmore Legend, NA/40			
Black Bowmore 1964/50			
Brackla	S	M	G
Royal 10/43			
Royal 1970/40			
Braes of Glenlivet	S	L–M	G
1979/cask strength			
8/62.6			
Bruichladdich	Islay	M	E
10/40			
15/40			
21/43			
25/45			
25/53.8 (Cadenhead)			
Bunnahabhain	Islay	L–M	G
12/40			
Caol Ila	Islay	L	E
12/40			
15/40			
1980/40			
Caperdonich	S	L–M	G
1968/40			
14/60.5			
Cardhu	S	L	S
12/40			
Clynelish	H	M–F	E
12/43			
14/43			
28/50.7			
Brora 1972/40			

Body: light (L), medium (M), full (F).   Regions: Highland (H), Speyside (S), Lowland (L).   Overall: superior (S), excellent (E), good (G), fair.

Name/Age/Strength	Region	Body/Rating	
An Cnoc 12/40	S	L	G
Coleburn 1972/40	S	L	G
Convalmore 1969/40	S	M–F	E
Cragganmore 12/40 Cask 1976/53.8 1974/40	S	L–M	S
Craigellachie 14/43 1974/40 26/46	S	M	G
Dailuaine 16/43 1971/40 22/46	S	M–F	G
Dallas Dhu 10/40	S	M	E
The Dalmore 12/40 30/54.5 Cooper's Choice, 24/43 Stillman's Dram, 26/45 50/cask strength	H	M–F	E
Dalwhinnie 15/43 27/45.5 1970/40	S	M–F	S
Deanston 12/40 16/55 17/40	H	L	G
Drumguish 3/40	S	L–M	G

Body: light (L), medium (M), full (F).   Regions: Highland (H), Speyside (S), Lowland (L).   Overall: superior (S), excellent (E), good (G), fair.

Name/Age/Strength	Region	Body/Rating	
Dufftown Glenlivet 8/40 10/40 15/43	S	L–M	G
Edradour 10/40 1968/46 1973/40	H	L	E
Fettercairn (Old) 10/43	H	L	G
Glen Albyn 1970/40	S	M	G
Glenallachie 12/40	S	L	G
Glenandrew 15/40	H	M	E
Glenburgie 8/40 1966/57.6 1970/40	S	L	G
Glencadam 1947/40 12/46	H	F	G
Glen Deveron 12/40 Macduff 1975/40 Macduff 12/55.5	S	L–M	G
Glendronach Traditional, 12/40 12/43 Sherry Casks, 12/40 18/43	S	M	G
Glendullan Pot-still Label, 12/43 Water-bird Label, 12/43 22/46	S	M–F	G

Body: light (L), medium (M), full (F).   Regions: Highland (H), Speyside (S), Lowland (L).   Overall: superior (S), excellent (E), good (G), fair.

Name/Age/Strength	Region	Body/Rating	
Glen Elgin NA/43	S	L–M	G
Glenesk 12/40	H	L–M	G
Glenfarclas Cask Srength, NA/60 10/40 12/43 15/46 17/43 21/43 25/43 30/43	S	F	S
Glenfiddich Special Old Reserve, NA/40 Classic, NA/43 Spode Decanter, 18/43 Wedgwood Decanter, 21/43	S	L	G
Glen Garioch 1984/40 12/40 15/43 21/43	H	M	E
Glenglassaugh NA/40 1983/40 15/59	S	L	G
Glengoyne 10/40 17/43 1968/50.3	H	L–M	G
Glen Grant 5/40 NA/40 10/43 Cadenhead's, 13/55.1	S	L–M	G

Body: light (L), medium (M), full (F).   Regions: Highland (H), Speyside (S), Lowland (L).   Overall: superior (S), excellent (E), good (G), fair.

Name/Age/Strength	Region	Body/Rating	
15/40			
15/46			
21/40			
23/46			
25/40 (Rating: Excellent)			
26/46			
1960/40 (Rating: Excellent)			
1964/46			
1965/40 (Rating: Excellent)			
Glenhaven	H	L–M	E
Aberfeldy, 17/59.8			
Ardmore, 18/59.3			
Benromach, 17/16.3			
Dalmore, 23/58.3			
Dufftown Glenlivet, 11/60			
Glen Albyn, 17/59.7			
Glendullan, 16/56.5			
Glenlivet, 17/65.5			
Glen Mhor, 12/64.2			
Glentauchers, 18/63.2			
Highland Park, 10/59.8			
Imperial, 18/60.3			
Macduff, 24/53			
Macallan-Glenlivet, 11/60			
Mannochmore, 17/63.3			
Glen Keith	S	M	G
10/43			
Glenkinchie	L	L–M	E
10/43			
21/46			
1974/40			
The Glenlivet	S	L–M	S
12/40			
18/43			
21/43			
George & J. G. Smith's:			

Body: light (L), medium (M), full (F).　Regions: Highland (H), Speyside (S), Lowland (L).　Overall: superior (S), excellent (E), good (G), fair.

Name/Age/Strength	Region	Body/Rating	
15/40			
15/46			
21/40			
1961/40			
29/52.2			
Glenlochy	H	L–M	G
1963/52.1			
1974/40			
27/46			
Glenlossie	S	L–M	G
10/43			
Glen Mhor	S	L	G
8/40			
15/40			
1965/40			
Glenmorangie	H	L–M	E
10/40			
10/57.6			
18/43			
21/43			
1972/46			
Port Wood Finish, NA/47			
Glen Moray	S	L	G
12/40			
15/43			
17/43			
1966/43			
1973/43			
Glen Ord and Glenordie	H	M–F	G
12/40			
Ord, 14/46			
Glen Rothes	S	M–F	E
8/40			
12/43			
1979/43			
Glen Scotia	H	F	S

Body: light (L), medium (M), full (F).   Regions: Highland (H), Speyside (S), Lowland (L).   Overall: superior (S), excellent (E), good (G), fair.

Name/Age/Strength	Region	Body/Rating	
14/40			
Glen Spey	S	L–M	E
8/40			
Glentauchers	S	L–M	G
1979/40			
17/46			
Glenturret	H	L	G
8/40			
10/57.1			
12/40			
"5,000 Days Old"/40			
15/40			
15/50			
1966/40			
1967/50			
1972/43			
Glenugie	H	L	G
1966/40			
Glenury Royal	H	L–M	G
12/40			
13/46			
14/43			
22/46			
Highland Park	Orkney	M	E
8/40			
8/57			
12/40			
14/55.2			
Imperial	S	M–F	G
1979/40			
Inchgower	S	L–M	G
14/43			
Inchmurrin	H	M	G
NA/40			
Old Rhosdhu, NA/40			
Inverleven	L	L–M	G

Body: light (L), medium (M), full (F).   Regions: Highland (H), Speyside (S), Lowland (L).   Overall: superior (S), excellent (E), good (G), fair.

Name/Age/Strength	Region	Body/Rating	
17/46			
1979/40			
21/46			
Isle of Jura	Jura	L	G
10/40			
10/63.9			
Limited Edition, 20/54			
Stillman's Dram, 26/45			
Kinclaith	L	L	G
1966 & 1967/40			
20/46			
Knockando	S	L	E
1966/43			
1976/43			
1977/43			
Ladyburn	L	L	Fair
20/46			
Lagavulin	Islay	F	S
12/43			
16/43			
Laphroaig	Islay	M	E
15/43			
16/57			
1974/55			
Linkwood	S	M	E
12/40			
12/43			
14/58.5			
15/40			
Littlemill	L	L–M	E
8/43			
22/46			
Lochnagar (Royal)	H	M–F	S
12/43			
Selected Reserve, NA/43			
Lochside	H	L–M	G

Body: light (L), medium (M), full (F).   Regions: Highland (H), Speyside (S), Lowland (L).   Overall: superior (S), excellent (E), good (G), fair.

Name/Age/Strength	Region	Body/Rating	
10/40			
Longmorn-Glenlivet	S	M–F	E
12/40			
15/43			
19/45			
1962/40			
1969/61.2			
The Macallan	S	F	S
Italian Market, 7/40			
10/40			
10/57			
12/43			
1975/43			
25/43			
Mannochmore	S	M–F	G
12/43			
Millburn	S	F	G
1971/40			
Miltonduff	S	M–F	G
12/43			
1963/40			
Mosstowie 1975/40			
Mortlach	S	M–F	E
15/40			
16/43			
21/40			
North Port	H	L–M	Fair
1974/40			
Oban	H	M–F	S
12/43			
Old Pulteney	H	L	G
8/40			
Pittyvaich	S	M	Fair
12/43			
Port Ellen	Islay	M–F	G
12/63.8			

Body: light (L), medium (M), full (F).   Regions: Highland (H), Speyside (S), Lowland (L).   Overall: superior (S), excellent (E), good (G), fair.

Name/Age/Strength	Region	Body/Rating	
13/43			
1974/56.4			
1977/40			
Rosebank	L	L	G
8/40			
12/43			
15/50			
St. Magdalene	L	L–M	Fair
1965/40			
Scapa	Orkney	M	G
8/40			
1963/40			
24/46.5			
1983/40			
The Singleton	S	M	E
1981/40			
Speyburn	S	M	G
10/40			
12/43			
1971/40			
Springbank	S	M	E
12/46			
15/46			
21/46			
25/46			
30/46			
West Highland 1966/58.1			
Longrow 1974/46			
Strathisla	S	M–F	G
8/40			
12/43			
15/40			
20/46			
35/40			
1958/40			
1960/40			

Body: light (L), medium (M), full (F).   Regions: Highland (H), Speyside (S), Lowland (L).   Overall: superior (S), excellent (E), good (G), fair.

Name/Age/Strength	Region	Body/Rating	
1967/40			
1980/40			
Strathmill	S	M–F	G
11/60.6			
Talisker	Skye	M–F	S
8/45.8			
10/45.8			
Tamdhu	S	L–M	G
8/40			
10/40			
15/43			
NA/40			
Tamnavulin	S	L	G
10/43			
20/46			
Teaninich	H	M	G
10/43			
17/43			
1982/40			
Tobermory	Mull of Kintyre	M	G
NA/40			
18/55.2			
Tomatin	S	M	G
10/40			
12/43			
1966/43			
1968/40			
Tomintoul	S	L	G
12/43			
Tormore	S	M–F	G
5/43			
10/40			
Tullibardine	H	M–F	G
10/40			

Body: light (L), medium (M), full (F).   Regions: Highland (H), Speyside (S), Lowland (L).   Overall: superior (S), excellent (E), good (G), fair.

Beginning in the 1980s, the Japanese entered the single-malt market. The Suntory distillery produced Yamakazi Pure Malt, Kioke Jikomi, and Kondaru. Other distillers offered Karuizawa and Hokkaido. Hardy Scots were bemused, a bit offended, but not worried.

The top ten single-malts in 1990s worldwide sales:

1. Glendfiddich
2. Glen Grant
3. The Glenlivet
4. Glenmorangie
5. Macallan

6. Cardhu
7. Cragganmore
8. Knockando
9. Springbank
10. Isle of Jura

How to Enjoy a Single-Malt

A single-malt should not be rushed in the drinking. Have it at room temperature (maybe with a splash of water) in a wine glass or snifter. Admire the color. Sniff the aroma. Sip slowly.

Scotch Blends

In 1905 the selling of a blend of grain and malted whiskey that had been made in a patent still got several pub operators in London's Borough of Islington in very hot water. Hauled into King Edward VII's court, they stood trial for serving "an article not of the nature and substance demanded."

The "substance" they called scotch was not a single-malt but a blend of several batches. The litigation was promptly called by Fleet Street newspapers the case of "What Is Whiskey?" Although the answer to the question arrived at by the court was in favor of single-malt, a Royal Commission (1909) issued an historic ruling. It declared: (1) the name *whiskey* should not be applied just to the product of the pot still; (2) whiskey is a spirit derived from the mash of *any* cereal grain or grains saccharified by the diastase of malt; (3) only such spirits distilled and bottled in Scotland could be called *scotch*.

Although more and more American scotch drinkers have taken an interest in single-malts, far and away the world's most asked-for scotches are blends. All but 2 percent of the combined output of Scotland's 120 distilleries—both malt and grain—are involved in blending.

Throughout the history of blending, experience taught that, as in human weddings, marriages in the world of scotch did not always work out. While one batch "married well," another that seemed to a blender to be ideal for commingling turned out to be the wrong mate. Blenders discovered that some whiskeys do not get along with others. Consequently, astute blenders know which of the whiskeys in what they call their library are best suited for blending. Creating a perfect blend is as tricky with whiskeys as in the making of perfume.

The process known as blending had begun in Scotland in 1853 when the Edinburgh firm of Usher, agents for Smith's Glenlivet label, mixed malts to make and market Usher's Old Vatted Glenlivet. Inspiration for blending whiskey came from the French. The process employed for whiskey is called vatting.

VATTING

The vat process begins with the selection of matured malt whiskey lying in casks in distillery warehouses. Each barrel is opened by a blender and nosed. If the contents meet the standards of the desired blend, they are poured into a huge vat. The mixed contents of several casks are left to stand open to the air. This is called marrying, and the process takes a year. Every blender has a particular recipe that is a closely guarded trade secret.

Although single-malts have to a great extent overshadowed vatteds, they still claim a niche, and there are excellent ones. They include Benmore, Berry's Highland Pot Still Liqueur and All Malt, Butler Royal, Campbell's Tomintoul Special 100% Vatted Malt, Cockburn's Pure Highland Malt and the Cockburn & Campbell Special, Duncraggan, Fine Fare (a British supermarket chain's own brand), Glen Blair, Glen Carren, Glen Isla, Glenleven, His Excellency, Mar Lodge, Royal Curloss, Seagram's Keith Classic, Strathspey, Whigham's, Gordon & MacPhail's Old Elgin and their "Pride of . . ." line—Pride of the Lowlands, Pride of Strathspey, Pride of Orkney, and Pride of Islay.

The most immodestly named vatted brand? "Greatness."

The most colorful names come from M. J. Mcdowdeswell & Co. in Britsol, England: Pig's Nose (four years old) and eight-year-old Sheep Dip.

One of the best known, Vat 69, got its name when its maker, William Sanderson, asked some friends to taste the whiskey from one hundred numbered vats and choose the best. They agreed on number sixty-nine.

Originally a maker of cordials, he took his personal credo, "Quality tells," and put it on the label. To guarantee supplies of high–class malts for his vats, he took over a distillery in the heart of the barley country of Aberdeenshire. Control of that company passed from father to son for several generations.

With vatting officially declared a way of making legitimate scotch, other individuals took the lead in promoting blending.

PIONEER BLENDERS

Except for automobiles, airplanes, women's fashions, and perfumes, no man–made product has been as closely identified with individual names as blended whiskeys.

Certainly, there are no more famous Scotsmen than those whose names appear on bottles of some of the most notable and popular scotch blends: Sanderson; John Haig; James Buchanan; James Whyte; Charles Mackay; Peter Mackie; John Begg; A. & A. Crawford; D. & J. McCallum; John McEwan; Arthur Bell; Seagar Evans; William Teacher; Hyram Walker; and William Whiteley.

A non–Scot, Samuel A. Bronfman, who launched Seagram's in Canada, got interested in scotch in the 1920s.

But there is one scotch blend that bears the most informal name on any bottle of scotch, whether single–malt or blended.

JOHNNIE WALKER

In Dashiell Hammett's novel *The Maltese Falcon*, published in 1929 and made into a movie in 1941—starring Humphrey Bogart as private detective Sam Spade and Sidney Greenstreet as the fat man Caspar Gutman—a crucial scene unfolds in Gutman's hotel suite. A rogue with a courtly style, Gutman wears a black cutaway coat, black vest, black satin ascot tie with a pinkish pearl, striped gray worsted trousers, and patent–leather shoes. The cigar he offers Spade is a Corona del Ritz. The whiskey is scotch in a tall glass with soda added from a siphon. When Spade lets him fill the glass, Gutman says, "We begin well, sir. I distrust a man that says when."

Taking the glass, Spade makes a little bow over it.

The fat man holds his glass against light through a window and watches the soda bubbles rise, then offers Spade a toast to "plain speaking and clear understanding."

As they talk about "the black bird," in Hammett's novel, their whiskey is identified by the author as Johnnie Walker.

While all the leading personalities who were present at the creation of scotch blends have interesting and inspiring stories behind them and their successes, the tale of John Walker and his family may be said to best embody the spirit (no pun intended) of the blended scotches.

The patriarch of family and firm started out in the early nineteenth century as a grocer in Kilmarnock, Ayrshire. Among his most popular commodities was his own brand of whiskey, Kilmarnock, named for the town. After the business was wiped out in a flood, he bounced back to become a goods wholesaler and quickly branched into the trade of supplier to shippers in the thriving port of Glasgow. He did so well that he opened an office in London in 1880. By that time, the major responsibility for the firm had devolved to his son

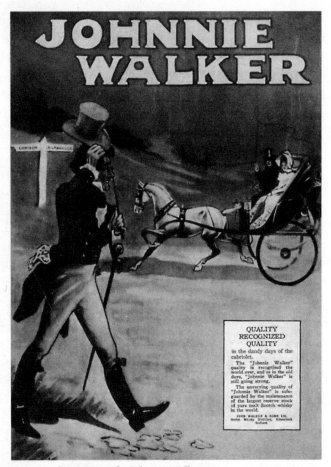

A 1911 advertisement for Johnnie Walker.
Courtesy New York Public Library

Alexander. It was he who in 1908 improved on Kilmarnock and renamed it in honor of his father. In association with a brilliant businessman, James Stevenson, it rapidly expanded into a whiskey empire. John Walker and Sons, Ltd. would market Johnnie Walker Red Label. It would become the world's favorite whiskey. Subsequent brands were Black Label; Gold, introduced on the hundredth anniversary of the company; and Blue, unveiled in 1993.

At the heart of the John Walker empire is a Speyside distillery at Cardhu. After maturing more than three years in sherry casks, at least forty grain and malt whiskeys are married with Cardhu single–malt. Bottling at 80 proof is carried out in the family's hometown in distinctively tall, square, tapering bottles with slanting labels. The figure of a striding man was added to the company's symbol in sentimental tribute to John Walker.

JOHN HAIG

Old archives show that Petrus von Hage, apparently descended from a knight who'd accompanied William the Conqueror across the English Channel from Normandy in 1066, received a royal grant in Bemersyde and promptly anglicized his name. But it was five sons of one of Petrus's heirs, John, who took up distilling in earnest as early as 1655. That year Robert Haig was very sternly rebuked by the local vicar for making whiskey on Sunday. One of the women in the family forged a link to Ireland by marrying the innovator of distilling in Dublin, John Jameson.

Doing business in the Lowlands, the Haig brothers and their descendants operated several distilleries. Finally headquartered in Markinch in 1877, the firm produced its standard brand, Haig, and the deluxe Dimple. For the United States market, facilities in Glasgow exported Haig and Haig and, in decanter–like triangular bottles with concave sides, Pinch.

JOHN BUCHANAN

Getting a taste for the whiskey trade by working for Charles Mackinlay & Co., merchants and blenders in London, John Buchanan was in his thirties when he struck out on his own. In forming the firm that bears his name, he introduced a blend in a black bottle with a white label, quite logically named Black and White. His skills at distilling and marketing soon made it possible for him to indulge a passion for owning Derby-winning racehorses. But it was another whiskey maker who put a horse on a whiskey label.

JAMES MACKIE

Trained as a distiller in Islay, James Logan Mackie took the name for White Horse from an inn at Edinburgh with a reputation as a spot where officers of "Bonnie Prince Charlie" relaxed during a rebellion in 1745. It was also from the White Horse that a daily stagecoach left Edinburgh for London, a rugged journey that took eight days—"If," as a traveler noted, "God permits." To get malt for his whiskey, Mackie turned to distilleries in the valley of the Spey and at Islay.

White Horse bottles were the first to have screw-top caps and a handle as part of the bottle.

JOHN DEWAR

Born in 1806, John Dewar began doing business as a wine and spirit maker in Perth in 1846. His distilling began in 1887 in a rented distillery in southern Pertshire. Nine years later, a new facility was opened on the River Tay and by 1923 the company had operations at Aberfeldy, Lochnagar, Muir of Ord, and Pulteney. Two years later the firm, along with the Walker and Buchanan companies, merged into the Distillers Company, Ltd. (DCL), organized in 1877 as a trade protective cartel.

JOHN BEGG

A close friend of Sanderson (of Vat 69), John Begg opened his distillery overlooking Balmoral Castle, the secluded summertime retreat of Queen Victoria. A pleasant and beneficial result of this location came in 1848 when the queen and her consort, Prince Albert, paid a visit to the distillery and pronounced it worthy of the prefix *Royal*. Consequently, Begg's whiskey was named Royal Lochnagar. For a time it was the most expensive drink in Scotland.

Black and White whiskey and its familiar faces, the black and white scotties.
Courtesy New York Public Library

WILLIAM TEACHER

Probably the youngest person to go into the whiskey trade, William Teacher was nineteen when he started a company in 1830. By age forty, he had eighteen licensed retail premises. Arguably the most popular of Teacher's labels was Highland Cream. So much of it was sold, with demand growing throughout the next century, that a new blending and bottling facility was built in 1962.

HIRAM WALKER

When Hiram Walker–Gooderham & Worts of Ontario, Canada, ventured into Scotland in 1930, it bought 60 percent of the Stirling Bonding Company and J. & G. Stodart, owner of Glenburgie–Glenlivet Distillery at Elgin, Speyside. Later Walker acquisitions included the venerable George Ballantine & Sons at Dumbarton and Miltonduff Glenlivet. All these long–established firms stood in the heart of a lush barley plain. Among Hiram Walker's most notable brands were Ballantine's, Old Smuggler, Rare Old Highland, and Ambassador.

"A LITTLE PRACTICE"

Perfection waits upon practice, just as genius needs infinite pains. Ceaseless care is ever taken to maintain the perfect maturity and perfect purity of —

DEWAR'S

A Dewar's advertisement from 1927.
Courtesy New York Public Library

SAMUEL BRONFMAN

To add his name to a long, distinguished roster of purveyors of scotch, in 1928 Samuel Bronfman bought control of the Joseph Seagram and Sons company, makers of American–style whiskeys in Canada (see Chapter Four). Seeking to break into scotch, the firm acquired one of Scotland's oldest distilleries. It also opened a new one, as well as developing its merchandising in connection with the old firm of Chivas Brothers.

Among Seagram's brands were Chivas Regal, Highland Clan, Sheriffs and 100 Pipers.

The first whiskey label to acknowledge abuse of alcohol, Seagram's implored users to drink moderately. An early advertisement asserted: "The real enjoyment whisky can add to the pleasure of gracious living is possible only to the man who drinks good whisky and drinks moderately. Whisky cannot take the place of milk, bread or meat. The pleasure which good whisky offers is definitely a luxury."

The objective of a blender is to produce a whiskey that, in the whole, is better than its parts—and to do so consistently week after week, year after year, so that there are no surprises for the drinker who chooses whiskey by the name on the label of the bottle.

All spirited drinks come in different sized bottles, measured by milliliter (ml). One liter equals 33.8 ounces; a quart is 32. In terms of liquor bottles that means:

ML	Ounces	Bottles per Case
50	1.7	120
200	6.8	48
500	16.9	24
750	25.4	12

Labels on bottles of blended scotch must by law state that the whiskey (spelled without the *e*) is a product of Scotland, that it is "100 percent Scotch whiskies" (note the plural), and the name of the distillery. Imports in the United States also carry the name and address of the importer. The strength of alcohol in a blend (carried on the label) is 80 proof.

As noted earlier, the age is the maturity of its youngest component, not the years of the blend itself. Pricing of a brand is generally a matter of age and quality of the malts, as well as the quantities of the brand available in the marketplace.

These are the 1990s' ten best-selling labels worldwide:

1. Jonnnie Walker Red
2. J&B Rare
3. Ballantine's
4. Bell's
5. Chivas Regal
6. Dewar's
7. Johnnie Walker Black
8. Grant's
9. Famous Grouse
10. Cutty Sark

Ironically (or perhaps not), the biggest consumer of scotch blends in the 1990s was the United States. The United Kingdom was second, followed by France, Spain, and Japan. Canada ranked sixteenth.

As to what to look for in a blended scotch, experts agree on these criteria:

» aroma: pungent, flowery, sweet, malty

» first-impression taste: peaty, smoky, sweet

» mouth-feel: smoothness, oiliness

» finish: how long does taste linger?

In evaluating a brand, look for the same quality you seek in a premium cigar or a restaurant: consistency. While brand loyalty is a virtue, experimentation is the very essence of excitement in living, so do not hesitate to sample the abundance of scotch in as many blends as are available.

While bearing in mind that it is the opinion of the author that there is no such thing as an unacceptable whiskey of Scotland, the following roster lists brands alphabetically and categorizes them good (G), excellent (E), and superb (S), on the basis of the author's experiences and a consensus of other evaluators, including ordinary consumers and connoisseurs, bartenders, liquor-store owners, and proprietors of drinking establishments. Not all may be easily available in the United States.

THE CHOICES

Brand	Rating	Brand	Rating
Abbott's Choice	G	Beneagles	G
Ainslie's	E	Benmore	G
Avonside	E	Ben Roland	E
Bailie Nicol Jarvie	E	Berry's:	
Ballantine's:		Berry's Best	G
Finest	E	Berry's All Malt	E
Founder's Reserve	S	Black & White	G
Gold Seal	S	Black Bottle	E
John Barr	G	Black Prince	E
Baxter's Barley Bree	G	Buchanan's	S
John Begg	G	Bulloch Lade	G
Bell's	E	Burn Stewart	S
Ben Adler	G	Cambeltown Loch	E
Ben Aigen	G	Catto's	E

Brand	Rating	Brand	Rating
Chairman's	G	El Vino	S
Chequers	G	The Famous Grouse	E
Chieftan's Choice	E	Findlater's Finest	G
Chivas Regal	S	First Lord (vatted)	S
Clan Ardroch	G	Fortnum & Mason	E
Clan Campbell	E	[The famed London provisioner's house brand]	
Clan MacGregor	G		
Clan Murdock	G	Fraser McDonald	G
Clan Roy	G	Fraser's Supreme	G
Clansman	G	Gairloch	G
The Claymore	G	Gale's	G
Club	S	Gamefair (vatted)	S
Cluny	E	Gillon's	G
Cockburn's Highland (vatted)	S	Glen Baren (vatted)	S
Corney & Barrow	E	Glen Calder	G
The Country Gentleman's	G	Glen Carren (vatted)	S
Crabbie's	G	Glen Catrine	G
Crawford's 3 Star	G	Glencoe (vatted)	S
Crinan Canal Water	E	Glendarroch	S
[Don't let the name inhibit you!]		Glendower (vatted)	S
Cumbrae Castle	G	Glen Flagler (vatted)	S
Custodian	G	Glen Garry	G
Cutty Sark	S	Glen Ghoil	G
[A classic!]		Glen Gyle (vatted)	S
Dalmeny	G	Glen Lyon	G
Peter Dawson	G	Glen Nevis	G
Derby Special	E	Glen Niven	G
Dewar's	S	Glen Shee	G
[A constant favorite in the United States since 1895]		Glenside	G
		Glen Stuart (vatted)	S
Dimple	S	Glentromie (vatted)	S
[It's Haig & Haig's Pinch in the United States]		Glen Urquhart	G
Diner's	E	Gold Blend	G
Doctor's Special	G	Gold Label	G
The Dominie	E	Golden Cap	G
Drambuie	E	Golden Piper	G
[Whiskey liqueur; see Chapter 13]		James Gordon's	E
Alexander Dunn (vatted)	S	Grand Macnish	S

Brand	Rating
William Grant's	G
Grierson's No. 1 (vatted)	S
Haig Gold Label	S
Hankey Bannister	S
Hart Brothers:	
Scots Lion	E
Dynasty Decanter	
(limited edition)	S
Harvey's Special	G
Heatherdale	G
Hedges & Butler Royal	G
High Commissioner	G
Highland Blend	E
Highland Clan	G
Highland Fusilier (vatted)	S
Highland Gathering	S
Highland Pearl	S
Highland Queen:	
Grand Reserve	S
Supreme	S
Highland Stag	G
Highland Woodcock	G
House of Lords	S
House of Peers	S
100 Pipers (Seagram)	E
[A world top-twenty seller]	
Immortal Memory	E
Imperial Gold Medal	G
Inver House (Green Plaid)	G
Islander	G
Islay Legend	G
Islay Mist (vatted)	S
Isle of Skye	S
J&B (Justerini & Brooks):	
Jet	S
Rare	S
Reserve	S
The Jacobite	G

Brand	Rating
King George IV	G
King Henry VIII	G
King James VI	G
King of Scots	S
King Robert II	E
King's Legend	G
Laird O'Cockpen	S
Langs	E
Lauder's	G
William Lawson's	E
Lismore	E
Logan's de Luxe	S
[Hard to find, even in Scotland]	
Lobard's	G
Long John	G
Lowrie's	G
William Low's Finest	G
MacAndrew's	G
MacArthur's	G
McCallum's Perfection	G
Sany Macdonald	G
McDonald's Special Blend	G
The (Stewart) MacDuff	G
MacKinlay (The Original)	S
Howard MacLaren	S
Sandy MacNab	G
Major Gunn's	G
James Martin's	E
Milner's Brown Label	G
Milord's	S
The Monarch	E
Monster's Choice	G
[A label that was around long before	
monsters in the movies]	
Muirhead's	G
Old Decanter	S
Old Elgin (vatted)	S
Old Glasgow	G

Brand	Rating
Old Glomore	G
Old Highland Blend	G
Old Inverness	G
Old Matured	G
Old Orkney	E
Old Parr	S
Old Royal	S
Old St. Andrews	E
Old Smuggler	G
OV 8	S
Passport	G
Peatling's	G
Pig's Nose	G
Pinch [U.S. version of Dimple]	S
Poit Dhubh (vatted)	S
Pinwinnie	S
John Player Special	S
Pride of... (vatted):	
Islay	S
Lowlands	S
Orkney	S
Strathspey	S
Putachieside	S
Queen Diana	E
[No relation to the Diana who married Charles]	
Queen Elizabeth	S
[Not to be confused with the brand sold in Abu Dhabi and South Africa]	
Queen Mary I	G
Queen's Choice	G
The Real Mackay	G
The Real Mackenzie	G
Reliance	G
Rob Roy	S
[Not to be confused with the cocktail]	

Brand	Rating
Royal Culross	S
Royal Edinburgh	G
Royal Escort	S
Royal Findhorn	G
Royal Game	G
Royal Household	E
Royal Salute	E
Sainsbury's (Own Label) [Store house brand]	E
St. James's	S
Scotia Royale	S
Scottish Leader [For supermarket trade]	G
Jock Scott	E
Sheep Dip (vatted)	S
Slaintheva	S
Spey Cast	S
Speyside	S
SS Politician	S
Stewart's Cream of the Barley	G
Strathbeg	G
Starthfillan	G
Superior Mountain Dew	G
Vat 69 (vatted)	E
Johnnie Walker:	
Red	S
Black	S
Gold	S
Blue	S
White & Gold	G
White Horse	G
Whyte & Mackay	S
William & Mary	E
Yellow Label	G
Ye Whisky of the Monks	G

Whichever type scotch you choose—a single-malt, a grain, a vatted, or a blended—the traditional toast is "Slainte" (pronounced *Schlan*-jer). May your experience please you, as it did the poet who alone one night in the glow of his hearthside wrote:

You have given me inspiration
For many a soulful rhyme—
You're the finest old scotch whiskey
I've had for a long, long time.

3

IRISH

"Give an Irishman lager for a month, and he's a dead man. An Irishman is lined with copper, and the beer corrodes it. Whiskey polishes the copper and is the saving of him."

—MARK TWAIN, 1835–1910,
Life on the Mississippi

Perhaps the root of the Irish style of drinking was summed up by nineteenth-century Irish playwright Dion Boucicault. On his deathbed, he said, "It's been a long jig, my boy, and I am only now beginning to see the pathos in it."

Certainly there was enough pathos in Ireland in a century of hard times when the Irish, seeking at least momentary relief from their travails, invented *uisge beatha*. An old Irish saying was: "May the pitcher be filled with spirited drink instead of water the next time you call to the house."

Distilling the water of life as a commerial enterprise, as noted earlier, began in the reign of King James I with Thomas Phillips's arrival on the shores of the Bush River in the northern province of Ulster's County Antrim in 1608.

West of Belfast on the northeast coast of Lough Neagh, the green rolling country offered good growing land, streams of pure water, and plenty of peat. It was choice whiskey country.

Charmed by the place and animated by a desire to obey King James by licensing distilleries, Phillips could not resist the temptation to cash in personally. Granting the first permit to himself, he launched with stroke of pen the first and longest-surviving name in Irish whiskey, Bushmills.

Bushmills

Deriving its water from St. Columb's Rill, a tributary of the Bush River, the firm triple-distills. This produces almost neutral whiskey that picks up its flavor from aging in sherry or bourbon casks. It consists of grain spirits with a touch of malt and is aged five to six years. In the 1990s the yearly output for both domestic and worldwide sales was about 350,000 barrels.

Unhappily, because Bushmills was made in Northern Ireland, a part of the United Kingdom whose people were subjects of the English monarchy—and the majority of them being Protestant—it fell victim to "the troubles" that tormented the people in Ulster, Protestant and Catholic alike, as well as in the predominantly Catholic Republic of Ireland, for centuries. The effect of this strife was to render Bushmills unwelcome in Irish Catholic pubs and bars, making it hard to get in certain parts of the United States, especially in the bars of Irish-American neighborhoods sympathetic to the slogan "England out of Ireland."

Once the favorite whiskey in the United States, Irish got a bad reputation during Prohibition. Much of the "hooch" peddled by bootleggers was passed off as "Irish," which

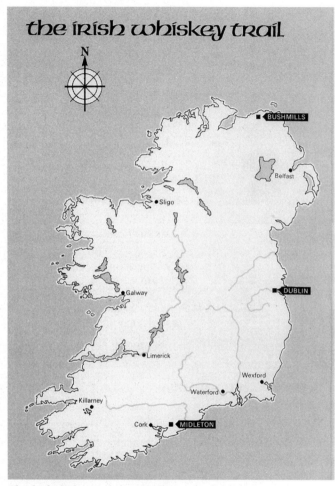

the irish whiskey trail

N

BUSHMILLS

Belfast

Sligo •

Galway •

DUBLIN

Limerick •

Wexford

Waterford •

Killarney

Cork • ■ MIDLETON

The chief whiskey-producing distilleries of Ireland.
Courtesy Irish Distillers Limited

Americans had liked before the dry spell. When a good deal of the faked stuff proved to be not just poor whiskey but possibly deadly as well, the tide of public opinion turned against the legitimate commodity when it became available with repeal. By that time, scotch and American-made Kentucky and Tennessee whiskeys—as well as gin—left all Irish distillers out in the cold in the lucrative U.S. market.

Through most of the twentieth century there were more than thirty distilleries in Ireland. The major ones were Bushmills, Andrew A. Watt & Co., Coleraine Distillery, Comber Distilleries Co., Cork Distilleries Co., Fitzgerald & Co., Jameson, Mitchell & Son, John Locke & Co., John Power & Son, Tullamore Dew Company, and the Midleton Distillery Co.

By the end of the century the ranks had thinned to a pair: Bushmills in Northern Ireland and Midleton in the Republic. But both are now operated by Irish Distillers Group, which is owned by a French beverage conglomerate, the Group Pernot.

59

All Bushmills and Jameson whiskeys are triple-distilled for smoothness.
Courtesy Irish Distillers Limited

BUSHMILLS BLENDS

Bushmills marketed two blends: Old Bushmills and Black Bush. The former was given nicknames by its devotees: Three Star, White Bush, and Red Bush. Many drinkers called it Ordinary Bush, which made its makers wince at the idea that a Bushmills could be anything but extraordinary.

Old Bushmills is a five-to-six-year-old blended grain with a touch of malt. It delivers the delicate flavor of honey, vanilla, and orange peel. If any drinker ever declared it, or any other Bushmills labels, less than superb, that individual has not been located.

There is also 1608 Bushmills Special Reserve, a twelve-year-old with a sherry character available only in duty-free shops.

BUSHMILLS MALT

Ireland's only single-malt, Bushmills Malt gets its barley from Northern Ireland's only commercial maltster and suppliers in the Republic of Ireland, Scotland, and France. The fermentation process results in a wash of 7.5 percent alcohol by volume (twice that of beer and ale). After being distilled three times, it is 80 percent alcohol by volume and is reduced to 63 for casking. At maturity (ten and sixteen years) the proof is lowered at bottling, to 40 for the ten-year-old and 58.6 in the twelve.

Bushmills is a very light, sweet drink with tones of grass and vanilla and a hint of sherry without peatiness. The color is deep amber with glints of gold.

For introduction in 1999 the company has planned "Millennium." A single-malt previously available only in fifty-three-gallon barrels, it is 1975 vintage, which will make it a

The cooperage at John Jameson's Bow Street Distillery, Dublin, circa 1920.
Courtesy Irish Distillers Limited

twenty–five–year–old malt when bottled in time for the arrival of the third millennium. Hence the name.

MIDLETON BRANDS

In addition to sharing in Bushmills' production of Black Bush and Old Bushmills, the modern Midleton complex at Cork in the Irish Republic blends Powers Gold Label, Tullamore, Paddy, Midleton Very Rare, and the second–oldest name in the history of Irish whiskey, Jameson.

All these are made with cereal/unmalted barley mash with a dash of malted barley. The resulting spirit has been described as nutlike, gentle, and warm, with the staying

Casks of Jameson Irish Whiskey being loaded for export shipment, circa 1920.
Courtesy Irish Distillers Limited

power for nursing a glass through an evening of conversation, or perhaps listening to recordings of sentimental Irish folksongs. Or, if your mood may be combative rather than contemplative, anthems and marching songs of the Irish uprising of 1916.

Although all Irish whiskeys can stand on their own in any setting, they are frequently mixed. Some of these drinks bear appropriately Irish names: Irish rose, Leprechaun, Irish driver, Irish rover, Irish handshake, four-leaf clover, and gloom lifter. (Some recipes are found in Chapter 10.)

It is safe to say that the way in which most Americans have come to know Irish whiskey is when it is mixed with coffee, sugar, and cream. They are rated below good (G), excellent (E), or superior (S).

THE IRISH WHISKEYS

Brand	Body/Character	Rating
Dunphy's	Light	G
John Jameson	Light, sweet	S
Murphy's	Light	E
Old Bushmills	Medium-light	S
Black Bush	Full	S
Paddy	Full	G
Powers	Full, barley malt	E

Irish Coffee

The story goes that the chef at Ireland's Shannon Airport, Joe Sheridan by name, spiced up cups of after-dinner coffee by slipping in slugs of Irish whiskey. This startlingly delightful concoction is said to have made its debut in the United States in 1952 at the Buena Vista Cafe on Fisherman's Wharf, San Francisco, where a plaque has been posted to commemorate the historic event.

Here's a basic recipe: Into a coffee mug (or a tall glass), pour hot coffee (the stronger the better); add a healthy spoonful of brown sugar; pour in one and a half ounces Irish whiskey; stir. Top it with a rich, chilled, double cream by gently pouring the cream onto a teaspoon that is held over the coffee. The cream spilling over the spoon should float. Do not stir it in.

The incomparable version at this author's favorite restaurant, Neary's (close to the corner of Fifty-seventh Street and First Avenue in New York City; no reservations required or taken; closed on Christmas; open on St. Patrick's Day only to regular customers, with Jimmy Neary controlling the door), is served in a tall glass with fluted sides, à la an ice cream sundae.

Some people take their Irish coffee iced. (It's enough to bring tears to these smiling Irish eyes.)

Irish Liqueurs

Invented in 1979 by R. & A. Bailey Co., Ltd., of Dublin, Baileys Original Irish Cream Liqueur quickly became the number-one-selling liqueur in the world—a million cases a year. Other brands include Carolans (number two in sales); Waterford, made by Irish Distillers International; O'Darby; Emmetts; and Irish Mist, said to be patterned on an ancient and long-lost recipe for Irish heather wine.

Because a major ingredient is milk, Irish liqueurs have been called milkshakes for grown-ups. Emmetts, for example, is 17 percent alcohol by volume. All Irish liqueurs are like wine, in that they should not be allowed to lie too long. They mix well with soda for a longer drink. Serve them cold, straight, or on the rocks. Other liqueurs are discussed in Chapter 13.

Proof that Ireland's invention of whiskey found acceptance by the Irish people may be found in Anthony Butler's *The Book of Blarney.* "Taking the country as a whole," he wrote, "there is about one public house or saloon for every sixty drinkers."

But in discussing drinking habits of an Irishman, social historian Mary Murray Delaney's *Of Irish Ways* noted, "In truth, he is not the most skillful drinker in the world."

Especially in America in the late nineteenth century, Irish were stereotyped as heavy drinkers. But in fact many belonged to temperance societies that bloomed as nineteenth-century Americans headed down the road into the twentieth century and the Volstead Act. This image of hard-drinking sons of Erin was the consequence of the instinctual need of the Irish to socialize publicly. While others preferred to do their drinking in private at home, Irish resorted to pubs in their homeland and in the saloons and bars of the cities of their fresh addresses in the United States.

"Be that as it may," continued Delaney, "the Irish had no trouble whatsoever finding an excuse for drinking. Some of them drank heavily to forget the disappointments of their lives. Others drank for the glory of life, for the glory of God, or to oil the machinery of their minds so that their thoughts might flow freely."

Summon the names of Irish authors and you will also conjure an image of hard drinkers:

An early Jameson advertisement shows Irish whiskey's fine reputation.
Courtesy Irish Distillers Limited

playwright Eugene O'Neill; poet Brendan Behan; novelist of the "lost generation" of the 1920s' Jazz Age, F. Scott Fitzgerald; novelist John O'Hara; and arguably the best writer on the topic of Irish American laborers during the Great Depression, James T. Farrell, in the novel *Studs Lonigan.*

Newspaper city rooms and press shacks connected to police stations also nurtured devoted drinkers, from today's Jimmy Breslin and Pete Hamill back to Damon Runyon of *Guys and Dolls* and Gene Fowler, biographer of New York's heavy–drinking mayor Jimmy "Beau James" Walker, and Broadway and Hollywood's notorious imbiber, "the great pro–file," John Barrymore.

Even longer ago was the Gay Nineties' social–commenting columnist Peter Finley Dunne, who spoke through his fictional philosopher–with–a–brogue, Mr. Dooley. Asked in *The Bar* by his friend Hennessy if drink is a necessary evil, Dooley replies, "Well, if it's an evil to a man, it's not nicissry, an' if it's nicissry it's an evil."

Although the peoples of the world have composed countless ways of offering a toast, the loquacious and literary–inclined Irish seem to have provided such salutes in greater number than others. (See Chapter 17 for a sampling of toasts around the world.) A favorite of this Irish writer goes: "May the Good Lord find you in Heaven a half an hour before the Devil realizes that you've gone."

That sentiment notwith–standing, when the times turned hard on the "Auld Sod" for Irish who were in no hurry to knock on St. Peter's Pearly Gates, the closest thing to Heaven on earth beckoned them from beyond the Atlantic Ocean.

THE GREEN GLENS OF ANTRIM

Far across yonder blue lies a true fairyland,
Where the sea ripples over the shingle and sand,
Where the gay honeysuckle is lurin' the bee,
And the green glens of Antrim are callin' to me.

And if only you saw how the lamp of the moon
Turns a blue Irish brae to a silver lagoon,
What a picture of heaven it would be;
Aye, the green glens of Antrim are callin' to me.
—Irish folksong

4

AMERICAN

"Oh, yer's yer good old whiskey,

Drink it down."

—BRET HARTE, 1836–1902,
The Men of Sandy Bar, 1876

More than a hundred years before the Statue of Liberty went up on Bedloe's Island in the harbor of New York to lift her torch to invite the world, in the words of Emma Lazarus's poetry, to "give me your tired, your poor, your huddled masses yearning to breathe free," the Northern Ireland port of Belfast was alive with ships carrying uprooted Ulster men, women, and children.

Bound to forge a new life for themselves in America, they did not leave whiskey out of their future. A quarter of a million came. Many took a mere passing look at the cities of the coast and proceeded westward, seeking patches of land for farming. They found it abundantly in the far reaches of Pennsylvania, Maryland, Virginia, and the Carolinas. Settled, they grew grains, and some of what they produced became a uniquely American drink from rye.

One of the popular pre-Prohibition brands in the United States was Golden Wedding, a Canadian whiskey marketed by Seagram.

Courtesy United Distillers Archive, Schenley Collection, Canadian Whiskey files

But upon the birth of the United States of America as a result of the revolution of 1776, conditions and circumstances changed. Partly because of taxation and the triumph of federalism in the form of the suppression of the whiskey rebels, and partly because of a natural wanderlust and curiosity as to what lay over the next hill, many of them again turned eyes to the west and the new territory, cut from Virginia in 1776, called Kentucky County.

Whiskey of these earliest days was known as "Western" and "Kentucky," to distinguish it from Pennsylvania and Maryland. With the creation of a new county where most distillers operated, their product became synonymous with the county's name. And so the rye that had gone west to Kentucky was reborn as bourbon.

Bourbon has flowed through the history of the United States like the Ohio and Mississippi rivers that carried it from Kentucky into the welcoming embrace of Americans in the years before the Civil War, by continent-spanning railroads on the opening of the West, and by train, plane, and truck in the twentieth century.

American-made whiskey played a role in the lives of the nation's elected officials. George Washington grew rye at Mount Vernon and turned it into rye whiskey. President Andrew Jackson served liquor in the White House, as did all the chief executives who succeeded him until Abraham Lincoln's time.

Whiskey figured prominently in Lincoln's life before and during the Civil War. Although "Father Abraham" was not reputed to be a drinker as president, he seems to have worked as a youth for distiller Wattie Boone near Knob Creek, Kentucky, before the Lincolns moved to Indiana. In addition to days of splitting logs and nights studying late by candlelight, Abe is said to have delivered food to his father at Boone's and ultimately done a little work there himself. Later, he even had his own license to operate a tavern.

During the Civil War, when he heard a complaint about the hard-drinking ways of battle-winning General Ulysses S. Grant, he suggested someone find out Grant's brand and have it supplied to the Union's other generals. Finally, John Wilkes Booth suffered a need to fortify his courage with whiskey in the Star Saloon near Ford's Theater a few minutes before he gave the United States its first assassinated president.

As everyone learned in school history classes, when General "Unconditional Surrender" Grant became president U. S. Grant, he maintained a generous supply of whiskey at hand during his two terms as the nation's chief executive.

During the Civil War, the thirst of soldiers in Grant's and Robert E. Lee's opposing armies led to the coining of a new word. Peddlers who tramped from camp to camp with liquor to sell by the drink carried their bottles in the tops of their boots. The troops called these welcome thirst quenchers "bootleggers."

Some sixty years later, bootlegging took on the sinister aspects of gangsters with colorful monickers—"Legs" Diamond, "Lucky" Luciano, "Owney" Madden, and "Scarface" Capone.

Occupants of the White House whose administrations bracket the years of Prohibition will be forever linked with liquor in our history books. Woodrow Wilson presided at 1600 Pennsylvania Avenue as Prohibition came in. Franklin D. Roosevelt campaigned for Repeal and welcomed it in the first year of his first term.

FDR also joined Britain's prime minister in hoisting glasses while planning defeats of the Nazis and the Japanese throughout World War II. How many whiskeys were gulped down in America and Britain celebrating the end of the war is beyond even a guess.

Harry S. Truman enjoyed bourbon while playing poker. Being an ex-soldier, Dwight D. Eisenhower was well acquainted with drink. John F. Kennedy was not only a partaker. Whiskey financed his education and lifestyle. His father, Joseph P. Kennedy, had made a fortune in whiskey during and after Prohibition.

Lyndon B. Johnson was notorious for invitations to political cronies to join him in "bourbon and branch" water in Washington and on his Texas ranch. Richard Nixon drank and, if you are to believe the tales that surfaced during and after the Watergate scandal, actually got drunk on duty. His successor, Gerald Ford, imbibed socially, although no one ever blamed his occasional fall down airplane steps or wildly hit golf balls on boozing.

Then came a brief respite from liquor in the White House under teetotaler Jimmy Carter. Note: *Teetotaler*, also *T-totaler*, derives from the pledge made by those in the heyday of the Temperance Movement who "swore off" consuming any sort of alcoholic drink, in contrast to others who left the door open to beer and wine. On lists of full- and part-time abstainers kept by abstinence societies, those who vowed to totally forswear all drinks were indicated by a *T* beside their names.

After Carter's ban on spirits, White House whiskey was again flowing for the guests of Ronald Reagan, George Bush, and William Jefferson Clinton.

Our history also records that almost since the founding of the nation, wheels of the Congress that turned to do the people's business on Capitol Hill were constantly lubricated with whiskey.

In other aspects of life in the United States, domestically produced liquor became "as American as apple pie." The annals of the U.S.A. are steeped in it. The language—as with *bootlegger* and *teetotaler*—has been made spicier by it.

The universal synonym for liquor—booze—may have been taken from the name of an 1840 Philadelphia whiskey man, E. G. Booz, who sold his in a bottle shaped like a log cabin. Some historians say that the word stemmed from the ancient Egyptian beer, *bouzah*. And English drinkers of long ago called their gusty drinking *bousen*, pronounced "boozen."

Speakeasy first appeared in the *New York Times* in 1895 as New York Police Commissioner Theodore Roosevelt reluctantly but dutifully enforced laws against the selling of alcoholic drinks on a Sunday. (He nearly got run out of office.) The word for a place for illegal boozing achieved nationwide currency during Prohibition, along with a new definition of *boot-leg*: It served as both noun ("This bootleg is very good booze") and verb ("I've got a friend who's risking getting pinched by the cops for bootlegging").

Although the word for illicit distilling of liquor in the United States is *moonshining* this description of making unlawful drink by the light of the moon is probably as old as the *uisge beatha* of old Ireland. The term took on its American flavor with the enactment of a whiskey tax in 1865. It drove many makers to set up illegal stills in the hills. The result was American moonshine and a new American folk character, the moonshiner "hillbilly." He was best exemplified in the comic strip *L'il Abner* in which the moonshine was "Kickapoo Joy Juice." In the era of television, a fictional Sheriff Andy Taylor and his bumbling deputy, Barney Fife, were constantly on the lookout for stills up in the hills around Mayberry, South Carolina. And no less an American television icon than the Waltons were conversant with moonshine in the persons of a pair of aging spinster ladies who sipped what they respectfully referred to as "father's recipe."

Surely, there is no more American figure than the lanky, leathery stranger who ambled into a saloon in a prairie cow town of the 1880s, hooked the heel of his boot on a brass

James E. Pepper founded his distillery in 1879 where his "Born with the Republic" Kentucky straight bourbon whiskey was made.
Courtesy United Distillers Archive, Schenley Collection, James E. Pepper files

bar rail, and ordered rye whiskey. In such an instance in American literature's first novel of the Wild West, Owen Wister's *The Virginian*, an otherwise nameless title character (played in the 1946 movie by Joel McCrae) retorted to a man who had insulted him, "Smile when you say that!"

The number of Western films with saloon scenes is probably incalculable. One of the least threatening by any critical standard has to be in *Destry Rides Again*, as a dance hall hostess/entertainer, played with saucy flirtatiousness by Marlene Dietrich, sang, "See what the boys in the backroom will have and tell them I died of the same."

Cowboy saloons ranged from hole-in-the-wall shacks to the rococo elegance of Dodge City's Long Branch. (Yes, it was a real saloon, not the work of the imagination of the writers of the television series *Gunsmoke*, although history books make no mention of anyone named Kitty as owner.)

Characters in the movies frequently referred to the liquor of the frontier as *rotgut*, and not without good reason. Mercifully, the whiskey of today is nothing like that of the era of gunslinging cowboys; not by a long shot. Because of years of experience by distillers, constant experimentation, refining innovations, and the industrialization of the making of it, the modern version is as close to the roughly hewn variety peddled on the frontier as today's smooth Irish and scotch are to those of King James's day.

Defining American Whiskey

The four types of whiskey categorized as "straight" American are rye, bourbon, Tennessee, and Canadian.

To qualify, they must be made using a method patterned after the Scottish style of carrying a portion of the backset of the first distillation to the next. This technique was improved in the United States in 1823 by an immigrant Scot, Dr. James Crow, who set about distilling the precursor of Old Crow Bourbon. The term in America for backset is *sour mash*.

Although sour mash does not appear on every American whiskey label, all brands are sour mash. The term has nothing to do with the taste of the finished product. Nor does *sweet mash* refer to flavoring. Unlike sour-mash whiskeys, a sweet mash is a whiskey made without taking some of the backset from the first batch and adding it to the next one to carry on and sustain the character of the distiller's product.

What Dr. Crow added to the process was the aging of the new whiskey in barrels whose insides had been burned to form charcoal, thereby *adding* both flavor and color.

American whiskey is distilled out at less than 160 proof (80 percent by volume) and is aged for a minimum of two years in new oak barrels whose interiors have been charred, with no flavor or color added. Alcohol that comes directly from the still in all American whiskeys is clear. Coloring is induced from the wood.

American blended whiskeys are a combination of straight and neutral-grain additives. (An exception is Tennessee whiskey, as defined and described later.)

BOTTLED IN BOND

To ensure consumers that what they were drinking was—and is—genuine American whiskey, President William McKinley in 1897 signed the Bottled-in-Bond Act. The law permitted whiskey makers to store their aging barrels in U.S. government-supervised warehouses, thus guaranteeing consumers that the whiskey had been rated 100 proof. This first-of-a-kind consumer-protection guarantee remains one of the laws governing whiskey making.

Subsequent statutes required that labels on bottles state whether the contents were "straight" whiskey or blended, as well as indicating age and proof.

Rye

Straight rye is made from a mash that contains at least 51 percent rye. This was the preferred whiskey of pre-Revolutionary War colonists. Its popularity waned in favor of bourbon.

The "Bottled in Bond" on this 1943 label of Old Fitzgerald bourbon meant that the whiskey was aged in warehouses supervised by the United States government under the Bottled-in-Bond Act. Signed by President McKinley in 1897 to ensure quality control, it was an early effort by the government to protect consumers against fraud.

Courtesy United Distillers Archive, Stitzler-Weller Collection, Old Fitzgerald files

Today's straight–rye labels include Jim Beam Rye, Old Overholt, Pikesville, and Wild Turkey. Canadian whiskey is also called rye.

Canadian

The story of spiritous drink in Canada paralleled that of the United States. The earliest European settlers made and drank rum. When later immigrants took up farming and found themselves with surplus grains, they started distilling. Soon whiskey replaced rum as the preferred drink of Canadians. In the eighteenth century there were about two hundred distillers. Today the number is down to a handful.

Canadian is produced only from cereal grains (wheat, rye, corn, and barley). Mashing, distilling, and aging follow the same general method as elsewhere. They are all blends, at least three years old by law (most are six). Although they frequently are called *rye*, this is incorrect. Canadian whiskeys contain no more rye than blends in the United States.

As noted earlier, an impetus for the debut in the United States of whiskey from Canada occurred in 1928 when Samuel A. Bronfman anticipated the inevitable ending of Prohibition in the United States by acquiring control of the major producer of whiskey and other spirits in Canada. Consequently, Seagram emerged and remained a familiar Canadian label on the shelves of U.S. bars and in liquor cabinets in American homes and offices. It seems quite unlikely that even a non–imbibing "man on the street" has not heard of or seen the tall bottles with pale yellow labels proclaiming *Seagram's V.O.* and *Seagram's Seven Crown*, the Sea-

O.F.C.

BON

A Whiskey You Know

The Pride of Old Kentucky "moves by name" that's the whiskey it pays to handle.

Once stocked you'll hear O. F. C. called for again. If you want a seller that satisfies, stock it.

In Bulk and Bottled in Bond

The Geo. T. Stagg Co. Inc.,
Frankfort, Ky.

Accounting and Sales Offices,
Rochester, N. Y.

The O.F.C. originally meant Old, Fire, Copper. When the company was taken over by the Canadian Schenley company, the public was asked to enter a contest to give new meaning to the letters. The winner was Oldest, Finest, Canadian.

Courtesy United Distillers Archive, Schenley Collection, Canadian Whiskey files

gram blend bottled in the United States. In pre– and post–World War II America, one of the most popular highballs was Seven Crown with 7UP. Logically named Seven and Seven, it still fares well.

The second great name in Canadian whiskeys is Schenley. But its history goes back to 1869 in Frankfort, Kentucky, where Pat Frazier built a distillery on the banks of the Kentucky River. The bourbon was called O.F.C. The initials stood for *Old, Fire, Copper*, meaning it was made the old-fashioned way, in copper stills over fire. In 1855 the company was bought by George T. Stagg. When he retired in 1892, the firm was taken over by Walter B. Duffy, who abandoned marketing O.F.C. by the barrel to sell it by the bottle. One of his innovations was introduction of the pint bottle. By 1910 the company had grown to a capital value of a million dollars. Nine years later it was put out of business by Prohibition, save for product stored in warehouses that was sold as "medicinal" whiskey.

This was carried out by the Schenley Distillery Company, which bought Stagg outright in 1929, along with the rights to O.F.C., Old Stagg, and Cream of Kentucky. The acquisition put Schenley in an advantageous position with repeal to become one of the "Big Four" distillers, along with National Distillers, Hiram Walker, and Seagram. By 1945 the firm was ready to enter the Canadian whiskey market. It did so by purchasing Quebec Distillers and changing its name to Canadian Schenley Ltd. A contest to choose a new meaning for O.F.C. was decided in favor of *Oldest, Finest, Canadian*.

Other Schenley acquisitions included the Finch Distillery in 1920, adding to Schenley labels an old and distinguished American brand, Finch's Golden Wedding Rye. It also took over the old Gibson Rye label, introduced MacNaughton Canadian whiskey in 1947, met a growing demand for Canadian whiskey by building a distillery in Vancouver, and gave MacNaughton an unmistakable Canadian identity by bottling it in a "Maple Leaf" decanter.

Canadian distillers and blenders include Arctic, Canadian Mist, Distillerateurs Unis du Canada, Distilleries Corby Limitée, FBM, Gilbey Canada, International Potter, Kittling Ridge, and Newfoundland Liquor. The whiskeys are Black Velvet, Canadian Club, Canadian Mist, Crown Royal and Crown Royal Reserve, and Seagram's V.O. Because of their delicate flavor, smoothness, and very light body, they are superbly suited for use in many mixed drinks.

Canada also produces London dry gin, Geneva gin, rum, vodka, brandy, and liqueurs.

Tennessee

The unique place of Tennessee in the history of American whiskey is the consequence of the experimentations of a curious fellow by the name of Alfred Eaton, a resident of Lincoln County, Tennessee, in the 1820s. Dickering with the process of making a whiskey the old way, he wondered what might be done to take the bite out of it.

The difference between the Tennessee process and that of bourbon making is that Tennessee is charcoal filtered. The charcoal is produced by burning stacks of oak. The charcoal is then placed in huge vats through which the distillate is filtered on its way to casking. Bourbon derives its flavor from oak casks that have had their interiors charcoaled by being set afire.   Courtesy Jack Daniel Distillery

He eventually tried dripping the distillate, before aging, into a vat through layers of charcoaled sugar–maple wood. The result proved delightfully mellow, and Eaton's way became known as the Lincoln County process. The taste has been described as "sooty–sweet."

Rather than using the before–aging, sugar–flavored charcoal–filtering method of the Lincoln County process, later makers of Tennessee filtered it after aging and just before bottling.

Because both these Tennessee methods added flavoring outside the cask, they diverged from the rule that the flavor of American whiskey must come only from the charcoaled insides of new oaken barrels.

But as whiskey historians and authors Gary and Mardee

Hadin Regan proposed in an article (*Malt* magazine, summer 1996 edition), "Think of it as a loophole that we should celebrate."

Tennessee whiskeys bear the names of two giants in the saga of American whiskey: Jack Daniel and George Dickel.

JACK DANIEL

Arguably one of the most famous names in the annals of American whiskey, he was known to family, friends, and business associates as Little Jack because he stood all of five feet five inches tall. He founded his namesake distillery in 1866 near Lynchburg, Tennessee. In the early 1880s he was joined in the business by a nephew, Lem Motlow. More than a century later, the company's motto reads, "Whiskey made as our fathers made it."

A likeness of Jack Daniel stands on the grounds of the distillery and is said to be the most photographed statue in all of Tennessee. If an individual ever exemplified the whiskey business simply through his physical appearance it would have had to be Gentleman Jack, with lush handlebar mustache and broad-brimmed, high-crowned, Western-style white hat.

A likeness of Jack Daniel stands on the grounds of the distillery and is said to be the most photographed statue in all of Tennessee.
Courtesy Jack Daniel Distillery

The Jack Daniel's square bottle with its white lettering on a black label is one of the world's most recognized. And the fine Tennessee whiskey within has always rated highly in esteem.

GEORGE DICKEL

Born in Germany in 1818, Dickel immigrated to the United States at the age of twenty-six and arrived in Nashville, Tennessee, in 1847. He got into the whiskey trade in 1861 and founded his own company in that city in 1870. With business booming, he built the Cascade Distillery in Tullahoma in 1879 and devel-

In 1938 George Dickel's Tennessee whiskey was available in "Powder Horn" bottles that were made for both right- and left-handed drinkers.
Courtesy United Distillers Archive, Schenley Collection, George A. Dickel files

oped one of the first brand names—George A. Dickel's Cascade Whiskey. Matured in new charred American white-oak barrels, it was advertised as being "mellow as moonlight." It remains so, delivering a clean, light, smooth, aromatic drink with a hint of sweetness.

Bourbon

In 1830 the English writer Thomas Carlyle observed, "History is the essence of innumerable biographies."

Eleven years after Carlyle penned *On History*, the American essayist Ralph Waldo Emerson was even more emphatic. "There is properly no history," he wrote in 1841, "only biography."

Just as the history of Irish and scotch can be found in the life stories of individuals, so may the development of whiskey in the United States be traced through the personal tales of very remarkable Americans whose names, and even some of their faces, appear on bottle labels, and many of whose names have become as familiar as those of the nation's founding fathers.

Furthermore, the whiskey business that these figures built in the United States is as much a part of the tapestry of American industry as the great names in automobiles, banking, steel, railroads, newspapers, broadcasting, movies, and computers.

In our era, names and pictures on packaging for a product are likely to have been the result of consumer research, public-opinion polls, and advertising-agency executives' brainstorming sessions. But in the world of whiskey it is far more likely than not that the name and occasional face on a label actually belonged to a real human being.

BOURBON PIONEERS

W. L. WELLER

After seeing action with the Louisville Brigade during the Mexican War, William LaRue Weller returned to the family farm in Nelson County, Kentucky, to join with his brother

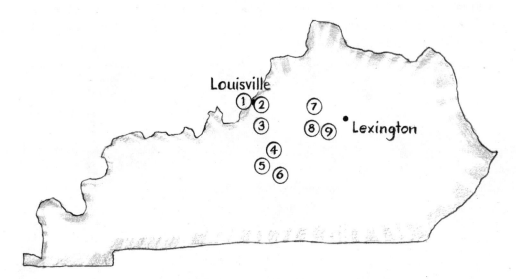

The bourbon distilleries of Kentucky: 1. Brown-Forman, 2. United Distillers, 3. Jim Beam, 4. Barton, 5. Heaven Hill, 6. Maker's Mark, 7. Leestown, 8. Four Roses, and 9. Boulevard. Map by Kevin Gordon

Charles in the distilling business that their grandfather Daniel had taken up nearly half a century earlier. Promising customers an "honest whiskey at an honest price," the grandsons organized the firm of W. L. Weller and Brother. By 1880 they were selling the drink "with a whisper of wheat" to steamboats, hotels, and taverns. With the death of Charles at the hands of a pair of bandits, the name of the firm was changed to W. L. Weller and Sons. The boys took over upon his retirement in 1896. He died three years later, but his name remains on the label.

OLD FITZGERALD

A salesman for the Wellers struck out on his own by taking over a distillery founded by John E. Fitzgerald, who had sold Old Fitzgerald to the steamboat and railroad dining-car trade. But it was Julian "Pappy" Van Winkle who took over the company during Prohibition and went on to guide the brand to true success by stressing quality. His slogan was "We make good bourbon at a profit if possible, at a loss if necessary, but we always make good bourbon."

Old Fitzgerald took pride in making its wheated bourbon from an expensive grain recipe, lower distillation levels, and a lengthy aging process, lending credence to the firm's advertising claim that it was the most expensive bourbon made in Kentucky.

The old bottling line of Old Fitzgerald distillery in 1905.
Courtesy United Distillers Archive, Stitzler-Weller Collection

Old Fitzgerald is now a product of the Bernheim Distillery of Louisville, Kentucky.

OLD CHARTER

The creation of Kentucky brothers Adam and Ben Chapeze Jr. in 1867, this sour-mash bourbon made from corn, rye, and malted barley was widely advertised as the bourbon "that didn't watch the clock." Because it was matured longer, Old Charter was a rich and full-bodied drink. No other bourbon is routinely sold at the ages of eight, ten, and twelve years.

Long before Colonel Sanders put himself on barrels of take-home Kentucky-fried chicken, Old Charter's brand employed the image of a "Kentucky colonel" and the slogan "Ask any colonel."

I. W. HARPER

The initials I. W. were those of Isaac Wolfe Bernheim. The *Harper* appears to have been a neighbor of Isaac and his brother Bernard, who when they started in the whiskey trade with one barrel of bourbon and life savings of twelve hundred dollars decided that the borrowed name was much more American-sounding than their own. A tradition-breaking move on their part was abandonment of selling bourbon in stone jugs in favor of glass bottles. Marketed since 1872, it is a traditional Kentucky straight sour-mash bourbon made from corn, rye, and malted barley and a protected strain of yeast. It is matured in new charred American white oak stored in brick warehouses.

America's leading premium export bourbon, and the best-selling bourbon in Japan, it is sold in 110 countries.

I. W. Harper also has the distinction of being the bourbon that was served at ceremonies opening the Brooklyn Bridge and the unveiling of the Statue of Liberty. It was the approved drink for the inaugurations of presidents Garfield, Arthur, Cleveland, and Harrison. I. W. Harper was acquired in 1937 by Schenley, which was itself bought by United Distillers in 1987. The Bernheims died in 1945.

MAKER'S MARK

Another manifestation of the persistence of family in the whiskey trade is found in Maker's Mark, whose tradition began when Taylor William Samuels began making whiskey in 1840. Except for the rude and calamitous intrusion of Prohibition, the work of distilling provided income for generations of the Samuels family. After whiskey became legal again, control of the struggling firm fell into the hands of investors. But bought back by the family in the 1950s, the firm is now run by seventh-generation bourbon distiller Bill Samuels Jr.

The Maker's Mark distillery nestles in a leafy hollow near Loretto, Kentucky, from which are shipped a limited number of handsome, slightly tapered, squarish bottles. They are sealed with hand-dipped bright red wax that dribbles down the long neck.

The "maker's mark" of Maker's Mark is an embossed-into-the-glass circle with a small star on the rim. The star signifies the Star Hill family site. It encloses the initials *S* and *IV*. The S is for *Samuels*; the *IV* represents the fourth-generation Samuels who developed the Maker's Mark recipe.

The whiskey is as elegant as the bottle, with tastes of oak, honey, and vanilla with overtones of raisins and spices and hints of cinnamon and nutmeg. Adjectives invoked to describe it have included lush, stylish, and sophisticated.

The output of the distillery is very small—twenty barrels per batch. The distillery with quaint old buildings was built in 1889 and is set in what one writer called "a storybook clearing surrounded by birch, walnut, oak, cherry, and sycamore." It is a Kentucky and National Historic Landmark.

HEAVEN HILL

Relative newcomers to bourbon, the Shapira family started Heaven Hill Distilleries shortly after Repeal when five brothers drew the first barrel in December 1935 on a chilly Friday the 13th. Evidently it was a lucky day. It now ranks as the eighth largest supplier of distilled spirits in the United States and the third largest holder of bourbon in the world,

The Heaven Hill Distillery at Bardstown, Kentucky.
Courtesy Heaven Hill

more than half a million barrels, or approximately 13 percent of all the bourbon on the planet. Its two leading brands are Heaven Hill and Evan Williams Kentucky Straight Bourbon, named for the man who opened the first commercial still in Kentucky in 1783.

A nearly disastrous day in Heaven Hill's history was November 8, 1996. Fire swept through the firm's offices and several of the warehouses containing thousands of barrels of bourbon. Fortunately, firefighters contained the inferno and saved many other buildings, permitting the distillery to stay in business.

JIM BEAM

The name on the bottle is that of the great grandson of Jacob Beam, who in 1788, the year the Constitution of the United States was ratified, loaded a secondhand wagon with all his goods, including a copper still, and followed Daniel Boone's footsteps through the Cumberland Gap into the bluegrass hills of Kentucky. Using his still to reduce the excess yield of his cornfields, he began making whiskey. He sold the first barrel in 1795. By 1811, as the whiskey market expanded (there were two thousand distilleries in Kentucky alone), Jacob, his wife Mary, and their twelve children had a thriving business in Washington County.

Inherited by son David in 1820, the Beam distillery moved in 1854 to take advantage of Kentucky's first railroad. The business settled beside a plentiful water supply in Nelson County and became known as the Clear Spring Distillery. At this point the third genera-

---

IF BY WHISKEY

"If by whiskey, you mean the Devil's brew, the Poison scourge, the bloody monster that defies innocence, dethrones reason, creates misery and poverty, yea, literally takes the bread out of the mouths of babes; if you mean the Evil Drink that topples men and women from pinnacles of righteous, gracious living into the bottomless pit of despair, degradation, shame, helplessness and hopelessness—then I am against it with all my power.

But if by whiskey, you mean the oil of conversation . . . that is consumed when good fellows get together, that puts a song in their hearts, laughter on their lips and the warm glow of contentment in their eyes; if you mean that sterling drink that puts the spring in the old man's steps on a frosty morning; if you mean that drink, the sale of which pours into our treasury untold millions of dollars which are used to provide tender care for our little crippled children, our pitifully aged and infirm and to build our highways and schools—then Brother, I am for it."

—Unattributed Pre-Prohibition Statement

Quoted by William Safire in His Column "On Language," *New York Times Magazine*, December 21, 1991

tion of Beams got into the business when sixteen-year-old James Beauregard began learning how to make whiskey. In 1894, at the age of thirty, he was running the firm, and would do so for the next half century. After weathering the great dryness between 1919 and 1933, he got back into the game at age seventy and incorporated the James B. Beam Distilling Co. in Clermont.

In 1946 his son, T. Jeremiah Beam, took the reins. Jim Beam died at the age of eighty-three the next year. During his tenure as master distiller, Jeremiah revived the firm's tradition of issuing commemorative bottlings, which had been started before the Civil War. These bottles generated a collecting craze and formation of "Beam clubs." Because Jeremiah was childless, the company passed into the hands of his nephew, F. Booker Noe Jr. On the two hundredth anniversary of Jacob Beam's founding of the family business, Booker Noe remained in command as the company's master blender and in that capacity introduced his own signature label, Booker's Bourbon.

Since the debut of Booker's, Jim Beam has also brought to market two other "ultra-premium small-batch" brands, Knob Creek and Basil Hayden. They joined a stellar list of products made and marketed by Jim Beam Brands Co., the second largest distilled-spirits company in the United States, with more than seventy spirits, including five of the thirty top-selling brands in the country.

MAKING BOURBON

While it may be claimed that the godfather of bourbon was Dr. Crow, the first of the rye whiskey makers who immigrated to Kentucky in the aftermath of the Whiskey Rebellion to discover charcoaling was the Reverend Elijah Craig. He put *corn* mash distillate into *charred* barrels in 1789.

What Crow and Craig discovered was that as the content of the casks sat, it absorbed through the charcoaled walls flavors of both charcoal and the underlying oak, as well as reddish color. A whiskey is bourbon only if made of at least 51 percent corn.

WHEATED

Whiskey made from mash that contains wheat rather than rye. The labels are Kentucky Tavern, Maker's Mark, Old Fitzgerald, Rebel Yell, Van Winkle, and W. L. Weller.

SINGLE-BARREL BOURBON

Single-Barrel Bourbon means what it says: The whiskey comes from one barrel. The number of the barrel usually appears on the label.

The maker of Blanton's Single-Barrel Bourbon described the process in advertising as an aging process in which each barrel is "strictly monitored" by a master distiller who determines precisely when the whiskey has extracted enough flavor from wood.

Other single-barrel bourbons are Elmer T. Lee, Hancock's Reserve, Rocky Hill Farms, Evan Williams (made by Heavenly Hill), and Wild Turkey Kentucky Spirit.

The latter brand started as the private whiskey served to guests by Thomas McCarthy, a New York gentleman who traveled every year to North Carolina for an annual wild-turkey shoot.

Aside from it being an outstanding example of straight rye whiskey, Wild Turkey catches the eye as readily as the palate. The bottle has ridged, arc-shaped shoulders that emulate the plumage of the wild turkey. The label is hunter green and depicts a wild turkey. The cap is pewter.

Small-Batch Bourbon

The term, coined in the 1980s by Jim Beam Brands Co., refers to a blending of whiskeys from casks that have matured at different storage temperatures and thus at different rates. It does not mean that only a small quantity was made.

Another small-batch maker is the A. Smith Bowman Distillery. Located near historic Fredericksburg, Virginia, it opened in 1935 in a distillery on Sunset Hills Farms, known today as Reston. Family-owned, it produces Virginia Gentleman bourbon and has lately branched out to imported scotch, Canadian, rum, and tequila and in the production of Bowman's Virginia vodka and gin.

Kosher

One of only two bourbons made outside Kentucky (the other is in Virginia) and the only kosher bourbon anywhere, Old Williamsburg Bourbon was introduced in 1994 by the Royal Wine Corporation of Brooklyn, New York. It has a medium body and a spicy, oakish taste. Kosher certification is a stamp on the back in Hebrew.

The Roster of American Whiskeys

The following American whiskeys are classified separately by type: bourbon, rye (blended), Tennessee, and Canadian. Within each type the brands are in alphabetical order. Body is noted as light (L), medium (M), or full (F). Overall impression (nose, taste, finish, color) is rated good (G), excellent (E), or superior (S).

BOURBON

Name	Body	Rating
Ancient Age	L	S
Ancient Ancient Age	M	S
Baker's (small batch)	L	G
Barclay's	L	G
Barton, Very Old	M	G
Jim Beam	M	S
Beam's Choice	M	S
Beam's Black Label	M	S
Beam 7-Year Reserve	M	S
Bellow's Club	M	S
Bellow's Rare	M	S
Bourbon Deluxe	M	S
Jacob's Well	M	S
Old Grand-Dad Bond	M	S
Old Grand-Dad	M	S
Old Grand-Dad 114	M	S
Old Crow	M–F	S
Old Taylor	M	S
Benchmark	M	G
Blanton's Single Barrel	F	S
Booker's (unfiltered)	F	S
Bowman's Virginia Gentleman	M	E
Colonel Lee	M	E
Elijah Craig	M	S
J. W. Dant	L	G
Eagle Rare	M–F	S
Early Times	M–F	E
Ezra Brooks		
Straight	M–F	G
Rare Old Sippin' Whiskey	M	E
Four Roses	M–F	S
Hancock's Reserve Single Barrel	F	S
I. W. Harper	M–F	S
Basil Hayden's	L–M	S
Heaven Hill	L–M	S

Name	Body	Rating
A. H. Hirsch (pot stilled)	F	S
J. T. S. Brown	M	G
Kentucky Gentleman	L	G
Kentucky Tavern (wheated)	M	G
Knob Creek	F	S
Elmer T. Lee Single Barrel	F	E
Maker's Mark (wheated)	F	S
Limited Edition	F	S
Mattingly & Moore	L	E
Henry McKenna	L–M	G
Tom Moore	L	E
Old Charter	F	S
The Classic 90	F	S
Proprietor's Reserve	F	S
Old Fitzgerald (wheated)	M	S
Bottled-in-Bond	M	S
1849	M	S
Very Special Old	F	S
Old Forester Bottled-in-Bond	M–F	S
Old Weller	M–F	S
James E. Pepper	L	E
Rebel Yell (wheated)	F	G
Rock Hill Farms Single Barrel	F	S
Ten High	L–M	G
Van Winkle (wheated)		
Old Rip Van Winkle Straight	F	S
Special Reserve Straight	F	S
Pappy Van Winkle Family	F	S
Virginia Gentleman (made in Va.)	M	E
Walker's Deluxe	L	E
W. L. Weller (wheated)	M	S
Old Weller Antique	F	S
Centennial	F	S
Wild Turkey	F	S
Old Number 8	F	S
Rare Breed	M–F	S
Kentucky Spirit Single Barrel	F	S
Evan Williams	L	S
Single Barrel Vintage	M	S

Name	Body	Rating
Yellowstone Kentucky Straight	M	G

RYE (Blended)

Name	Body	Rating
Beam's 8 Star	L	S
Bellow's Reserve	M	S
Calvert Extra	M	S
Kessler Blend	M	S
Mt. Vernon	M	S
Old Overholt	F	E
Partner's Choice	M	S
Pikesville Supreme	L	G
PM Blend	M	S
Sunnybrook	M	S
Wild Turkey Straight Rye	F	S

TENNESSEE

Name	Body	Rating
Jack Daniel's Tennessee Sour Mash		
Old Time No. 7 (black label)	L	S
No. 7 Brand (green label)	L	S
Gentleman Jack	F	S
George Dickel Tennessee Sour Mash		
Old No. 8	F	S
No. 12 Superior	F	S
Special Barrel Reserve	F	S
Lem Motlow (Jack Daniel's)	F	S

CANADIAN

Name	Body	Rating
Black Velvet	L	E
Canadian Club	L	E
Canadian Mist	L	E
Crown Royal	L	E
Lord Calvert	L–M	E
Seagram's		
V.O.	L	E
Seven	L	E
Schenley O.F.C.	M	S
Schenley V.O.	L	S
Windsor	L	S

PART II

WHITE
GOODS

5

GIN

*"If only my kith
And all of my kin
Were as much fun to be with
As I am on gin."*

—ANONYMOUS

Of the European cities that contributed to the history of the United States one of the least heralded is the Dutch seaport Leiden. It was from there in 1620 that members of an oppressed English religious sect who called themselves Puritans set sail on the trim ship *Mayflower* for the New World, thereby being recorded in elementary school history books as the Pilgrims. But thirty years later in that same city in Holland a professor of medicine at Leiden University discovered something that was destined to please and have a profound effect on descendants of millions of immigrants who followed the Pilgrims to America.

The clever Dutch doctor was Franciscus de la Boe, also known as Dr. Sylvius. His discovery was to become known and admired in the entire world as gin.

In addition to becoming the basic ingredient of America's most popular drinks, gin helped fuel Prohibition–era bootlegging mobsters, speakeasies, women imbibing alcohol in public, and the cocktail party. Like whiskey, but even more so, the spirited drink created in a Dutch laboratory in hope of giving the world a medicine injected the language of liquor with colorful words and apt phrases: gin mill (bar or saloon), bathtub gin (bootleg alcohol), gin disposal unit (drunkard), and ginned (inebriated).

Gin also provided generations of dramatists, screenwriters, songwriters, comedians, and cocktail–party conversationalists a lot of fodder for their wit. An example from a 1996 syndicated newspaper column by Ann Landers: "Water is composed of two gins, oxygin and hydrogin. Oxygin is pure gin. Hydrogin is gin and water."

What Dr. Sylvius discovered as he searched for a medicine to treat sailors of the Dutch East India Company for various tropical maladies was the benefit of the juice of the juniper berry as a tonic. He found that when it was added to alcohol it worked as a sedative, diuretic, vasodilator, and appetite stimulator. He gave it the name *aqua vitae*, the Latin for "water of life."

Nobody but doctors thought of it as medicine.

Sylvius's countrymen drank it because they liked it. They called it *jevener*, the Dutch word for "juniper." To the French the berry was *genièvre*, which in English became *geneve*, then *gin*.

British troops who encountered it during military forays into the Netherlands in the seventeenth century promptly coined it "Dutch courage" and smuggled gallons of it home with them.

Always a people to recognize a good thing, as they'd noted the salutary properties of Irish and scotch whiskeys, the English started making their own. But with a difference. The Dutch alcohol used in making gin was distilled from barley and aged. This gave Dutch gin a malty flavor. But as a result of the Act for the Encouraging of the Distillation of Brandy and Spirits from Corn (1690), Britain's was distilled from corn and not aged. This gave English gin a lighter body with the crisp taste of the added juniper. The style took its name from two English cities, Plymouth and London. But it is made elsewhere, including the United States.

The Ginning of America

Dr. Sylvius's drink reached the Western Hemisphere courtesy of Dutch seamen who dropped anchor in New Amsterdam and helped in the creation of the tradition of a hard-drinking place that continues in the image of New York as the city that never sleeps. While the preferred drinks of Manhattan's first settlers were beer and rum, gin was soon holding its own.

Author John Kobler in his history of drinking and the temperance movement in America, *Ardent Spirits*, wrote, "In New York the breakfast beverages were likely to include . . . genever—Dutch gin, colloquially called strip-and-go-naked . . ."

The inhabitants continued the drinking after England's King Charles II sent his army to wrench New Amsterdam from the Dutch and hand it over to his brother James, Duke of York, who renamed the place after himself.

But it took another three centuries before gin catapulted into the realm of popular spirits in the United States to rival whiskey in nightclubs and private parlors of Americans as the basis of mixed drinks. In 1996 *The Complete Bartender* by Robyn M. Feller listed 258 drinks made with gin. But it was one gin drink that achieved such reverence that this book devotes a whole chapter to it: the martini (Chapter 11).

What about gins makes them different? How are they made?

London gins are three quarters corn and one fourth barley combined with water to form a mash for fermenting, then distilled by the Aeneas Coffey patent-still method. The end product is 180 proof (90 percent alcohol). This is reduced to 120 proof by adding distilled water. It then goes in a gin still, a modified pot still developed by James Burroughs, founder of the Beefeater brand. To the still are added the juniper and other flavorings.

The home of Plymouth gin is the Black Friars Distillery, built in 1425.
Courtesy New York Public Library

The brands include Beefeater, Bombay, Boodles, Booth's, Burnett's, Cork, Gordon's, Mr. Liquor, Seagram's, and Tanqueray.

Plymouth gin, made only in Plymouth, England, by Coates & Company, is a little heavier and rounder than London gin.

Scheiden (Holland) gin, primarily made in its eponymous Dutch town, is distilled from mash that is equal parts barley, corn, and rye. The result is a whiskey–like flavor.

THE GIN GLOSSARY

Gin: An alcohol distilled from grain and flavored with juniper berries and other botanicals, including anise, bitter almonds, cardamom, caraway, cassia bark, calamus, cocoa nibs, lemon peel, licorice, orange peel, and orrisroot in small amounts. Gin is colorless or with the slight yellow tint of straw. Although it is generally sold at 80 proof, it may be found in the United States as high as 94.

Dry Gin: A gin that is not sweetened.

Flavored Gin: Sweet gin flavored with orange, lemon, or mint.

Geneva (also Holland and Scheiden): Dutch gin. Highly flavored and not well suited for mixing.

Golden Gin: A dry gin aged in wood.

Vacuum-Distilled: Distilled in a glass–lined vacuum still at a low temperature (90 degrees, rather than 212 degrees), thereby collecting only the lightest, least bitter flavors and aromas.

Pink Gin: A combination of Plymouth gin and angostura bitters said to have been invented by sailors of the British navy as a cure for various seagoing–related illnesses. It didn't work, but it produced a drink with an exceptional kick.

Old Tom: Gin sweetened for use as a liqueur.

Sloe Gin: A liqueur flavored with sloes instead of juniper (see liqueurs, Chapter 13).

THE GINS

Name/Country/Proof	Body	Rating
Ancient Age/U.S./80	Medium	S
Beefeater/England/94	Medium	E
Bellows/U.S./80	Medium	S
Bombay/England/86	Full	E
Brigadier/U.S./80	Medium	S
Calvert/U.S./80	Medium	S
Dark Eyes/U.S./80	Medium	S
Fleischman's/U.S./80	Medium	G
Gilbey's/U.S./80	Medium	S
Gordon's/U.S./80	Full	S
Hiram Walker/U.S./80	Medium	E
Kamchatka/U.S./80	Medium	S
Plymouth/England/94.4	Full	S
Seagram's Extra Dry/U.S./80	Medium–Full	E
Tanqueray/England/86	Medium	E

Rating: G, good;   E, excellent;   S, superior.

6

VODKA

"It is the Russians' joy to drink; we cannot do without it."

—THE PRIMARY CHRONICLE, 1377

Wthen James Bond sprinkled pepper into a glass of estimable Wolfschmidt vodka to the astonishment of M, his boss and head of British secret services, Agent 007 smiled sheepishly and explained, "In Russia, where you get a lot of bath-tub liquor, it's an expected thing. Now it's a habit."

The addition of the pepper was intended to settle some of the unpleasant oils found in poorly made Russian vodka.

Furthermore, as everyone knows, Bond never accepted anything from Russia with love.

Although vodka is assumed to have originated in the Russia of the fourteenth century, there is compelling evidence to argue that it came from Poland. The word *vodka* is a corruption of the Polish *zhizennia voda,* or "water of life." (There's that phrase again!)

A second assumption about vodka is that it is made from the potato. But its primary ingredient is wheat, although it can be and is made from any kind of food plant, including corn, rye, and beets. And, yes, potatoes.

Its association by Americans with Russia seems to stem from the introduction of the name of Smirnoff onto the United States liquor stage in 1939 when the right to put "Smirnoff" on a label was acquired by the firm of Heublein. But it was not until 1946 that vodka began making a noticeable dent in Americans' zeal for whiskey and gin. As noted by John J. Poister in *The New American Bartender's Guide,* this was because World War II had left liquor-store shelves stripped of nearly every kind of liquor.

"In those days vodka was known only vaguely," Poister wrote. It was the beverage in Chekhov plays, Tolstoy novels, and in films about cossacks and Karamazovs. Definitely not American!

During the war, soldiers of the Red Army got drunk from it. Joseph Stalin supposedly gulped gallons.

But at war's end, thanks to Heublein's prewar foresight, abundant supplies of Smirnoff were available to Americans for the first time. To fuel demand, a brilliant slogan was launched. To an inexplicably mouth odor–conscious nation the ads exclaimed, "It leaves you breathless."

Finally, the Smirnoff exponents offered a recipe for a vodka drink—Moscow mule. It consisted of Smirnoff vodka, half a lime, and ginger beer. Americans went crazy for it.

These clever exploitation ploys, the acute liquor shortage, and a preoccupation with anything Russian came in the warm glow of Soviet-American alliance against Nazi Germany and before war-weary Americans realized that they were about to be forced to confront the questionable intentions of Soviet communism.

Soon, like James Bond, who preferred vodka in his martinis in Ian Fleming's Cold War thrillers, Americans found little to love about Russians, except their potent, crystal-clear liquor that did, indeed, leave them breathless.

By the end of the 1960s it had passed gin in popularity and a decade later had supplanted whiskey in the public-opinion polls that asked Americans their favorite spirit.

Making Vodka

The liquor may have been invented in Poland, but it was a Russian chemist, Andrey Albanov, who refined the formula. In 1810 he developed a charcoal-filtration system that removed impurities that remained after distillation in a manner similar to that of all the spirited drinks. As in making gin, the difference between vodka and whiskey is that vodka is not aged.

United States law requires vodka's neutral, charcoal-filtered spirits to be "without distinctive character, aroma, taste, or color." Consequently, vodka is ideal for use in mixing, not only for James Bond's martini, but in a vast variety ranging from Bloody Mary to White Russian.

Vodkas of the World

RUSSIA

Once upon a time in czarist Russia there were four thousand makers attempting to seduce Nicholas and Alexandra from their favorite Smirnoff. This rampant form of capitalism went by the boards with the communist revolution, but vodka would remain the national drink from Moscow to Siberia.

With the ending of the Cold War, the collapse of the Soviet Union, and a rebirth of capitalism, new Russian brands abounded.

Among the most famous of the Russian vodkas, Stolichnaya is made of glacial waters from Lake Ladoga, north of St. Petersburg. The distillate is filtered through quartz and activated charcoal. The vodka is known affectionately as Stoli. There are numerous flavored versions. Limonnaya (guess!) is 80 proof, good on the rocks and in lemony drinks; the peppery 90-proof Okhothcniya is known as "hunter's vodka" and is much like a liqueur. Other flavors include vanilla, coffee, cinnamon, and peach.

Pertsovka is 70 proof, dark amber in color, and aged in wood. Its spicy character goes very well in a Bloody Mary.

Tarkhuna is made with the herb of that name that grows in Georgia (not the one in the United States, but the home region of the late boss of the USSR, Josef Stalin). It is light green in color and a rather gentle drink.

Entering the American premium-vodka market in 1990, Cristall vodka is distilled from winter wheat. The body is creamy. Food and drink commentator Anthony Dias Blue's *The Complete Book of Mixed Drinks* called Cristall the Château Lafite of the vodkas. (Author's note: knowing Andy as I do—I was his boss at a New York radio station for a couple of years—this kudo was not given lightly.)

Among the artful series of vodka ad campaigns is this one for Stolichnaya's new vodka, Millennium.
Courtesy Carillon Importers, Ltd.

Recognizing the long, sad history of politics and government in Russia, the most thrillingly named Stolichnaya vodka in the new Russia has to be Freedom (40 proof).

When you drink it, think of Stalin's gulags, James Bond, and the Berlin Wall.

POLAND

Three years before Christopher Columbus stumbled upon the Americas, the people of Poland were drinking a rye vodka that they called *Wodka Wyborowa*. They still are. It is a soft, lush drink in 80 and 100 proof with a smooth texture.

Actually made from potatoes, Poland's Luksusowa is triple-distilled and delivers a very smooth experience.

With the name Belvedere, you might suppose the vodka in the bottle with a many-columned mansion on the label would be English, but it is made in Poland of 100 percent Polish rye. It has a creamy smoothness.

NORWAY

The firm of Heublein produces the Smirnoff name that it obtained from the Russian family, as well as Finlandia and Vikin Fjord. Finlandia is an exceptional vodka in a silvery bottle with a black label and a trio of white deer racing beneath the midnight sun of Finland.

SWEDEN

Although the Swedes also have been making vodka for hundreds of years, the brand that was introduced to Americans in 1985 is Absolut. Now ranked among the best-sellers in the United States, it gives the consumer a choice of 80 and 100 proof, great for mixing and on the rocks. Absolut Citron is lively lemony; Absolut Kurant has the taste of black currants; Absolut Peppar carries the jolt of jalapeño and paprika.

DENMARK

At 80 proof, Denaka made its American debut in 1991, in a clear, triangular bottle. The contents are 100 proof with a soft and creamy body and caramel-vanilla flavor. Denaka 101 may be in a black bottle but it's a bright drink.

HOLLAND

Imported to the United States by Heineken, Krimskaya is 80 proof with a smooth body and slightly herbal taste that is best on its own, or chilled and straight up.

In the making of Ketel One, as in scotch, the middle cut of the distillate is used. This fine vodka is smooth and pure.

ICELAND

What else would you call a drink from Iceland but Icy?

Relatively new in the competition for the vodka drinker's heart, it is 80 proof, silky and dry, and comes in a nifty clear flask with a silver cap.

AUSTRALIA

The name on the label is Bushman's. The vodka is as hardy and straightforward as folks Down Under. Enough said, mate!

ENGLAND

From the most famous name in English gins, Beefeater, comes Burrough's English Vodka. Distilled from corn and barley, it is filtered through fine oak from Sussex. Spicy and rich, it is best neat or on the rocks.

Tanqueray Sterling, made by Tanqueray gin people, is double–distilled and filtered over granite. The bottle is the shape of the gin container, but frosted. Complex and elegant.

CANADA

Leaving no portion of the world market up for grabs, Seagram provides 80 proof Seagram's Imported Vodka. Its intense flavor is enjoyable straight and complementary to mixers.

JAPAN

From Suntory Company, originated in 1899 as a wine maker, Suntory vodka is sold in a square bottle adorned with Japanese characters and elegantly drawn trees. In 80 proof, the vodka is smooth and dry. The 100 proof is intense.

UNITED STATES

Out of Anchorage, Alaska, Attaskia is 80 proof and made with glacier water. It delivers a dry hint of vanilla and finishes in a hint of spice.

A New World drink with an Old World vodka name, Smirnoff is 80 proof; Silver Private Reserve is 90.4, with creamy/silky body, and dry mouth, with a little bite of spice at the finish.

Introduced in 1993, Skyy rocketed into the stratosphere of sales by 1995. Triple–filtered, it is freer of impurities than any vodka.

Another popular American vodka is 80–proof Georgi (with the "r" in the name backward to suggest the Russian alphabet). At a popular price, it is a smooth, clear drink.

And there is Wolfschmidt (80 proof), providing all the best of vodka with no need to emulate James Bond by sprinkling it with a little pepper.

Because of the soaring popularity of vodka, as well as the relative ease in making it, new vodkas appear with astonishing regularity. One that came on the market in 1996 from the Sazerac Company of Los Angeles—Rain—was promoted as meeting "high standards of environmental conservation" because it was made from organically grown grain and sold in a recyclable package with the bottle labels and cases made from recycled paper, "a first in the beverage industry."

No matter how many there are, it continues to be a liquor that lends itself to mixing (recipes in Chapter 10).

POPULAR VODKA RATINGS

Brand/Country	Rating
Popov (U.S.)	Superior
Stolichnaya (Russia)	Excellent
Tanqueray (U.K.)	Excellent
Bowman's (U.S.)	Fine
Smirnoff (U.S.)	Fine
Georgi (U.S.)	Good
Gordon's (U.S.)	Good
Stolichnaya Cristall (Russia)	Good
Rain (U.S.)	Good
Suntory (Japan)	Good
Vladimir (U.S.)	Good
Absolut (Sweden)	Good
Wolfschmidt (U.S.)	Good
Finlandia (Finland)	Fair
Gilbey's (U.S.)	Fair
Icy (Iceland)	Fair
Zyntia (Poland)	Fair

"BOND. JAMES BOND."

Here is a recipe for a martini invented but not given a name by the debonair secret agent who invariably introduced himself as "Bond. James Bond."

3 measures of Gordon's gin
1 measure of vodka (grain, not
 potato)
½ measure Kina Lillet (French
 aperitif, white)

➤   Shake very well until ice cold. Add a large thin slice of lemon peel. Serve in deep champagne goblet.

While enjoying it, look out for those sneaky SMERSH agents!

7

RUM

"Yo-ho-ho, and a bottle of rum."

—ROBERT LOUIS STEVENSON,
1850–94, *Treasure Island*

ere's the timeless drink of the bounding seas, our Founding Fathers, 1920s boot-leggers, and the hot-blooded and joyous people of an island of blue skies, turquoise waters, sparkling beaches, and palm trees—Puerto Rico.

Finding a place they considered a doorway to the riches of the Americas, fifteenth-century Spaniards arrived, took over, and named it accordingly. When the conquerors tasted a native drink, they took an immediate liking to it and its effect, and called it *aguardiente.*

By 1672 an English visitor could write home to a friend about Puerto Ricans, "They make a sort of strong water they call Rumbullion, stronger than spirit of wine."

In traditional English fashion, the name of the sugarcane libation was quickly short-ened to *rum.*

But it was not until 1865, when Don Sebastian Serralles left his home in Catalonia and took with him a French pot still to the island that Puerto Rico produced a rum commer-cially. He named it Don Q. It is still being made and it is the number one rum in Puerto Rico, as well as its leading export.

As noted earlier, the making and trading of rum provided one leg of the rum–slave triangle formed by the Caribbean Islands, New England, and Africa. The rum that stayed in America—called New England or Yankee—became a popular commodity in taverns by the names Kill Divil, Bogus, Rattle-Skull, and others equally as rustic. But rums also came up from the islands of the Indies.

In an edition of Benjamin Franklin's *Poor Richard's Almanac,* one read:

> *"Boy, bring a bowl of china here*
> *Fill it with water cool and clear;*
> *Decanter with Jamaica ripe . . ."*

By 1817, rum was being consumed in New York at every hour of the day. But with the ending of the slave trade after the Civil War and the increasing popularity of whiskey as America's drink, rum drinking receded. Not even annexation of Puerto Rico in the 1898 Span-ish–American War could revive it as the preferred drink in the United States. Whiskey still reigned supreme and was easy to get, until the Volstead Act shut down domestic distilleries.

Suddenly the nefarious sea-lanes between the West Indies and the continental United States of the old rum–slave trade triangle returned to use. In big ships and small, loaded with illicit whiskey and outlawed rum, men who plied the coastal waters became known as rumrunners. The route followed between one dropping–off point at Atlantic City, New Jersey, and New York was Rum Row.

Despite these names, American drinkers still showed little zest for rum itself. Prohibition's clampdown on the availability of whiskey failed to elevate rum as a serious competitor for the affections of the parched people of the United States.

The stature of rum was not even bolstered by the 1940s hit song that touted the joys of "drinking rum and Coca–Cola."

This dislike was in large measure because quality standards for making rum did not exist. The rum that was offered simply was not a very pleasing thing to drink.

In an attempt to stave off economic ruin, the Puerto Rican government's post–World War II Mature Spirits Act

Mexico was a nearby source for rum during Prohibition.
Bettman Archives

imposed a strict code for making rum. The law required that rums be aged at least a year and blended so as to produce a light, dry drink free of impurities, harsh oils, and aldehydes. Furthermore, to ensure that rums made elsewhere were consistent with the improved Puerto Rican variety, any country wishing to copy the method was invited to do so without having to pay for the know–how.

Making Rum

The significant difference between distilling whiskey and rum is that the basic ingredient of rum, sugarcane, does not have to be first turned into a mash in order to produce fermentable sugar, as must be done with cereal grains. The juice of sugarcane is converted to molasses. A small batch receives an infusion of yeast, which is allowed to work for a week to ten days. This is mixed with non-yeasted molasses in a fermentation tank. Seventy-two hours later, the contents are placed in continuous-column patent-style stills. These steam out alcohol of very high proof and purity.

After aging in American oak barrels, the rum is married to other batches of varying ages to produce the color, aroma, flavor, and body desired by the bottler. There are three types classified by color: white/light, gold/amber, and dark. A fourth type has its flavor enhanced with spices.

The minimum age in years and body type are as follows:

Type	Age	Body
white or light	1	light
gold or amber	3	medium
dark	5–7	full
spiced	3–4	light–medium

Light rums are made in Cuba, the Dominican Republic, Haiti, Puerto Rico, and the Virgin Islands. Full rums may be found in Barbados, Guyana, Jamaica, Martinique, and Trinidad. Spiced rums come from Java in Indonesia, but more and more American rums are also being made available in flavors, primarily citrus. Most rums are 80 proof, though some go as high as 151 proof.

Standardization of distilling contributed to rum's ascendency as a drink all over the world, with economic benefits for the countries making and exporting it.

The New World of Rum

More than a century and a third after Don Sebastian Serralles brought his pot still to Puerto Rico, his Don Q brand was still ranked as a popular export. But it found itself competing in a worldwide market with both its immediate Caribbean neighbors and other Latin American countries.

Rated fair (F), good (G), excellent (E), or superior (S), brands offered by major rum-making countries are:

Country	Brand	Rating
Antigua	Cavalier	G
Barbados	Alleyne Arthur's Special Old	E
	Cockade Fine	E

Country	Brand	Rating
	Cockspur	E
	Gosling's Choicest	S
	Lamb's Navy	E
	Lightborn's Selected	E
	Old Brigand	S
	Mount Gay Eclipse	E
	Mount Gay Sugar Cane Brandy	G
Bermuda	Gosling's Black Seal	G
Colombia	Ron Caldas	F
	Ron Medellín	F
	Tres Esquinas	F
Costa Rica	Ron Viejo Especial	F
Cuba	Casa Merino 1889	E
	Havana Club	E
	Ron Matusalem	E
Dominican Republic	Barcelo	G
	Bermúdez	G
	Brugal	G
	Macorix	G
	Siboney	G
French West Indies	Rhum Bally	G
	Rhum Clement	G
	Rhum La Mauny	G
	Rhum Negrita	G
	Rhum Saint-James	G
Guyana	Lemon Hart & Sons Memerara	F
	Hudson's Bay Demerara	F
Haiti	Rhum Barbancourt	F
	Barbancourt Rhum Liqueurs	F
Jamaica	Appleton	E
	Coruba	E
	Daniel Finzi Fine Old	E
	Gilbey's Governor General	E
	Hudson's Bay Jamaica	E
	Kelly's	E
	Captain Morgan	E
	Myers's	E

Country	Brand	Rating
	Rumona Jamaica Rum Liqueur	E
	Skol	E
	Wray & Nephew	E
Panama	Abuelo	F
	Carta Vieja	F
	Cortez	F
Puerto Rico	Bacardi	S
	Carioca	S
	Castillo	S
	Boca Chica	S
	Don Q	S
	Grenado	S
	Llave	S
	Myers's Rum	S
	Ron Merito	S
	Palo Viejo	S
	Ronrico	S
	Ron del Barrilita	S
	Ron Matusalem	S
	Trigo	S
St. Lucia	Jos. Jn. Baptiste Crystal	G
	Clear White Rum	G
St. Vincent	Sunset St. Vincent	G
Trinidad	Fernandes Vat 19	G
	Ferdi's 10-Year	G
	Old Oak Rum	G
	Siegert's Bouquet	G
Venezuela	Cacique Ron Anejo	F
Virgin Islands, British	British Navy's Pusser's Rum	E
Virgin Islands, U.S.	Cruzan	S
	Old St. Croix	S
	Poland Spring	S
	Ron Chico	S
	Ron Popular	S

Although rum is fine on its own, its role in the world of high spirits, like that of gin, has been as the chief ingredient in mixed drinks. There are hundreds of rum drinks with colorful names encompassing the alphabet from Acapaulco to zombie (popular recipes may be found in Chapter 10).

Mixed or straight, throughout history rum has earned a place of respect right next to gin. But no spirited drink, including John Barleycorn as the nemesis of temperance campaigners, was dragged to the depths of political rhetoric as was rum. It took place when Samuel Dickinson Burchard led a deputation of clergy to call on Republican presidential candidate James G. Blaine in 1886. Assuring Blaine they would not follow others who threatened to break away from the Grand Old Party, the preacher thundered, "We are Republicans, and don't propose to leave our party and identify ourselves with the party whose antecedents have been Rum, Romanism, and Rebellion."

On the other hand, England's Lord Byron, in taking up his talented pen, found nothing amiss in a combination of Heavenly Spirit and a flagon of rum. "There's nought, no doubt, so much the spirit calms," he wrote, "as rum and true religion."

American poet Richard Hovey took somewhat the same tack when he wrote of Eleazer Wheelock, a very pious man who went into the wilderness "to teach the Indian." His sassy ironic ode concluded:

> Eleazer was the faculty, and the whole curriculum
> Was five hundred gallons of New England rum.

Another Byron, Byron Rufus Newton, included the drink in his assessment of New York City in 1909:

> Purple-robed and pauper-clad,
> Raving, rotting, money-mad;
> A squirming herd in Mammon's mesh,
> A wilderness of human flesh;
> Crazed with avarice, lust and rum,
> New York, thy name's Delirium.

Throughout history no other spirit has provided literature and the popular arts such romantic imagery as rum. Certainly, no more exciting and colorful figures exist in English letters than the pirates of Robert Louis Stevenson's rousing *Treasure Island,* with their rousing chanty, "Fifteen men on the Dead Man's Chest; yo–ho–ho and a bottle of rum."

That rum has been associated with seafarers dates to the age when men who went down to the sea embarked under sail, whether as pirates, explorers of the Spanish Main, or the "tars" who voyaged and warred under the ensign of the British crown. In Britain's navy since the reigns of Henry VIII and Queen Elizabeth I, each man was entitled to a daily ration of grog. It got its name after the "grogman" cape that Admiral Edward Vernon wore when he cut rations of rum by adding water to keep crewmen from getting drunk. To pirates who sailed the briny deep on the ships of Henry Morgan, grog was rum mixed with scurvy-preventing lime juice.

To show that times had not changed between reigns of two British queens, whenever Elizabeth II disembarked from the royal yacht *Britannia* after a voyage, her order to hand out rations of rum as reward to the crew was a term that had been around as long as rum grog and the Royal Navy: "Splice the main brace."

8

TEQUILA

"Take another shot of courage."

—LYRIC FROM "TEQUILA SUNRISE"
BY D. HENLEY AND G. FREY,
RECORDED BY THE EAGLES.

Tequila! The very name sends the mind tripping through so many memories, personal and collective, to other names. History's Santa Ana and his *federales* arrayed against Davy Crockett and Jim Bowie at the Alamo. Black Jack Pershing leading American soldiers in marauding raids south of the border hunting for the desperado Pancho Villa. The movies' Humphrey Bogart in the guise of Fred C. Dobbs, desperate for cash in a dusty saloon in *Treasure of the Sierra Madre*. The bandito in the big sombrero, his wide mouth full of bad teeth, bellowing "Ba'ches? We dunt need no stinkin' ba'ches!" And the grossly bloated Orson Welles in *Touch of Evil* as the corrupt sheriff who waged a campaign of terror against Charlton Heston in a scruffy Mexican border town in which Marlene Dietrich now *owned* the cantina. So many cowboy movies had guys drinking tequila that trying to recall titles would be futile.

With the possible exceptions of tacos, tortillas, burritos, and marijuana, nothing conjures up Mexico in the American imagination so readily as the country's ancient national drink. But before tequila came *pulque*.

Spirits of Agave

When Spain's *conquistadores* moved onward from the islands of the Caribbean onto the mainland to take over the land of the Aztecs they found the inhabitants drinking yet another potent potion which they called honey water (*aguamiel*). Made from juice of the maguey plant, *pulque* was fermented and drunk immediately in the manner of beer. With introduction by Spaniards of distillation, two new drinks appeared, mezcal and its much more refined relative, tequila.

Though the maguey plant family has more than four hundred varieties, it is only the blue agave version that is harvested and processed to distill the spirit that takes its name from the small town in the heart of the agave region near Guadalajara in the state of Jalisco.

Maturation of an agave plant takes ten years. Only the heart is used. Chopped, shredded and cooked into a pulp, it is pressed for its juice. With or without sugarcane added, the fermentation is done in huge stainless steel vats and lasts four days. To up the proof it is double-distilled in a copper pot still. The result is a white ready-to-sell 80 proof tequila that is comparable to gin and vodka. With a distinctive peppery flavor it is called both white and silver. Gold tequila (the color is more amber than gold) is aged in oak barrels for at least a year, giving a more robust quality. All shades of tequila are well suited for mixing.

The names are as lively as drink and country, ranging from Brave Bull and Caramba to TNT (tequila and tonic) and Zorro. One of the best known is the margarita (recipes in Chapter 10).

But this "exotic" drink differs from others in an important way. With tequila there is a "macho" way to down it.

Tequila Pancho Villa Style

To achieve the proper effect the tequila ordered should be the white non–aged variety poured into a manly glass. A delicate martini chalice just won't do. The bartender will supply a little pile of coarse salt and a wedge of lime. You will also require a chaser called *sangrita*. A mixture of tomato and orange juices, it contains chiles and onions (recipe in Chapter 10).

Pile some of the salt on the fleshy web between your thumb and forefinger. Lift that hand and the one holding the glass of tequila to mouth level. Lick off the salt and quickly gulp the tequila. Suck the lime wedge. Follow with *sangrita*.

When you catch your breath, you may feel an urge to call the fire department or ambulance. Don't! Your image is on the line.

A less flamboyant alternative is to drink the tequila from a glass with salt–encrusted rim, with lime and *sangrita* optional.

Tequila Choices

Among the best available in the United States and marketed in white and gold are Beamero, Jose Cuervo, Sauza, and Tempo.

Attuned to an increasing number of Americans whose economic status allowed them to investigate the single–malt scotches and premium cigars, Jose Cuervo launched a big advertising campaign directed at persuading them that Cuervo tequila deserved to be in the picture with the fireplace, leather chair, and fine cigar. One full-page magazine ad offered Reserva de La Familia de Jose Cuervo of 100 percent agave and aged three years in oak casks and advised it be "sipped and savored, much as one would a fine cigar or single–malt scotch."

Other brands sold in the United States: Centinela (100 percent agave); Chinaco; Dos Reales Gold; Gusano Rojo; Herradura Anejo, Silver and Gold; Montezuma; Patrón Anejo and Silver; Porfidio; El Tesoro and Anejo Silver.

Further evidence of the rise of tequila's popularity was found in an invitation from an establishment primarily devoted to beers. New York City's Heartland Brewery (calling itself "The Classic American Brewpub") offered a "Tequila Festival" that it promoted as "an evening of *divertido especial*" at which one might "party" on eight super-premium tequilas and learn how to make the world's best margarita. All this while being serenaded by a live Mariachi band. Other inducements were "Shooter Girls and Caballeros," an assortment of Mexicali appetizers, and a *piñata* raffle. The price was thirty-five Yankee dollars a person.

Mezcal

Mezcal (or mescal) is also made from agave, but it can be produced from any variety of the plant. A much cruder product, its bottle may have a maguay worm in it, put there to give the drink a reputation as a "man's drink." (The worm is *never* found in genuine tequila. But should there be a worm that has made its way into yours—and survived—the *sangrita* chaser is certain to kill it.) Consuming the worm with your mezcal will do no harm to your stomach and health. What it may do for your *macho* image is for you to decide.

PART III

MIXOLOGY

9

THE PERFECT BAR

For people like Lou Grant, the iras-
cible television news director on The Mary
Tyler Moore Show, *the perfect bar was the
bottle of whiskey and glass he kept in the
bottom drawer of his desk.*

*The one you set up in your
home or office will depend on
how grand you want it to be;
how complete your inven-
tory of liquors is or will be; and,
of course, how much you want to
pay for all it takes to furnish your ideal layout.*

If you're to be a proficient bartender there are a few words you'll have to know to avoid looking like an amateur:

Absinthe	A liqueur. It doth not make the heart grow fonder. See Chapter 13.
Amaretto	A cordial. See below and Chapter 13 for this and other cordials.
Aperitif	A before-meal liquor of any kind, but usually one mixed with vermouth or bitters. A cocktail.
Armagnac	See Chapter 12.
B&B	Mixture of cognac and Benedictine. See Chapter 12.
Beer	See another book.
Bitters	See Chapter 12.
Brandy	Distilled grapes. See Chapter 12.
Chaser	An after-drink drink intended to take the edge off whatever preceded it.
Cocktail	A chilled spiritous drink. If you didn't know this, you probably do not belong in back of a bar. Or in front of one.
Collins	A tall liquor drink usually mixed with soda and something fruity.
Cooler	A collins made with wine.
Cordial	A liqueur. See chapter 13. Also the way to be when tending bar.
Daisy	An extra-large cocktail of rum, gin, or other white liquor, sweetened with fruit syrup and served over crushed ice.
Dash	A small amount, about ⅛ teaspoon.
Drop	As in "I'll have a drop of scotch." It usually means "fill 'er up."
Eggnog	Christmas made merrier with a mixture of sugar, milk, and egg yolks in bourbon, rum, or brandy.
Fix	A sour cobbler made with lemon, sugar, and any liquor over crushed ice.
Fizz	A bubbly concoction of a citrus drink, sugar, soda, and gin (or wine).
Flip	Creamy mixture of eggs, sugar, a citrus drink, and a liquor.
Frappé	Pronounced "frap-aay," and "frap," it is a glass filled with crushed ice over which you pour liquor. In Boston, a frappé is what everyone else calls a milkshake.
Garnish	Item added to a drink—an olive, for example.
Highball	Tall spiritous drink with approximately 1½ to 2 ounces liquor and 10 ounces of a mixer. A lowball is a short drink.
Jigger	Small amount of liquid, about equal to the capacity of a shot glass, around 1½ ounces.

Julep	Bourbon, sugar, and mint leaves, dahling!
Lemon wheel	A fancy way of garnishing with lemon. A slice is cut a quarter of the way and hung on the rim of the glass.
Mist	A glass of ice with liquor poured over.
Neat	A glass of liquor with nothing added. Also called straight.
On-the-rocks	A small glass of liquor and ice cubes.
Pony	One ounce—a shot glass.
Proof	Either the alcoholic content of a drink or valid evidence that a person has attained the legal age for drinking.
Punch	All the liquor you have goes into a bowl with some kind of juice and fruit slices floating on top. Spiked punch has been jazzed up with liquor, usually surreptitiously and mischievously in old movies starring Mickey Rooney, Dead End Kids, or the three old army sergeants in the John Wayne movie *Fort Apache*.
Shot	A thumb-sized, one-gulp glass of liquor. Contents of a shot glass. A pony.
Shooter	A spirit poured directly into a glass from a bottle. Also a strained drink.
Sling	Tall glass with liquor, lemon juice, and sugar topped with club soda.
Sloe Gin	Note that it is not a "slow" gin. It is not even gin, but a liqueur made with sloe berries, from the blackthorn bush.
Smash	A julep in an old-fashioned glass.
Sour	Liquor and the juice of lemon or lime in a short glass, usually an old-fashioned.
Swizzle stick	Something with which to stir your drink. May be made of paper (a straw) or plastic, carried home from some fancy bar. Many people collect them. The swizzle was originally a rum drink.
Toddy	Made with any spirit. It used to be only made with hot water ("hot toddy") but is now also served cold with soda and spices.
Tonic	Tall glass, tonic water, gin or vodka.
Virgin	A mixed drink, minus the spirit.
When	As in "Say when," meaning to tell the bartender when to stop pouring. Never trust anyone who doesn't know when to say when. Confiscate his car keys.
Wine	See another book.

The Fully Equipped Bar

These are the recommended implements for use in preparing and serving drinks at a completely oufitted bar:

Bar spoon	Long handle (ten inches) with a muddler (a thing at the other end for mashing).
Blender	Electric, for mixing stuff and crushing ice. Bottle and can opener(s).
Bowls	For sugar. Salt for rimming tequila glasses.
Corkscrew	The simpler the better.
Cutting board	Watch out for your fingers.
Double-ended measure	Metal with a small cup (1½ to 2 ounces) at one end and a pony (1 ounce) at other.
Fruit peeler	A paring knife will do.
Funnel	Always recommened in "how to be a good bartender" books, though I have yet to grasp the need for one.
Glassware	See below.
Grater	For preparing fixings of some mixed drinks.
Ice bucket	Big enough to hold your largest bottle.
Ice pick	If you get your ice by the block.
Ice scoop	Using your hands is a no-no.
Measuring cup	Kitchen type.
Measuring spoons	Kitchen type.
Napkins	Little paper ones, often with snappy or witty sayings and/or cartoons printed on them. And coasters if you really want to be fancy.
Pitcher	For pouring mass-produced drinks.
Shaker	Usually made of metal, looks like the big metal cup from a milkshake mixer.
	A "Boston" shaker is in two parts: a large glass in which the liquids are poured for mixing and a slightly wider stainless cap of equal capacity that is fitted over the glass. Both are then shaken to accomplish the mixing. To learn how, rent the movie *Cocktail* and watch Tom Cruise.
Squeezer	For fruit.
Strainer	Metal mesh disk surrounded by springy metal coils that fit over the tops of glasses. It's called a Hawthorn.
Stoppers	For closing bottles.

| Toothpicks | To stick in the olives in martinis or into other garnishes. |
| Water pitcher | To hold water for mixing drinks. |

Glassware

Balloon	Large bowl, 10 to 14 ounces. Excellent for margaritas, other cocktails, wines.
Beer Mug	With a handle. Also called a stein.
Cocktail	Wide mouth, sloped sides, stemmed, 3 to 6 ounces.
Collins	A 10- to 14-ounce cocktail glass.
Highball	Straight sides, 8 to 10 ounces.
Old-Fashioned	Short, straight sides, 8 to 10 ounces; perfect for wrapping your fist around.
Pony	Small, up to 2 ounces.
Shot	Ditto.
Sour	Short and fancy with fluted sides for fancy drinks; 5 to 6 ounces.
Snifter	Short, stemmed. For cognacs, brandies, liqueurs, and wines.
Tulip	Taller version of the snifter.

Measurements

Drop	A drop
Dash	2 or 3 drops
Teaspoon	⅙ ounce
Tablespoon	½ ounce (3 teaspoons)
Ounce	2 tablespoons
Pony	1 ounce
Jigger	½ to 2 ounces; 3 to 4 tablespoons
Cup	8 ounces
Pound	16 ounces (2 cups)
Pint	16 ounces (2 cups)
Quart	32 ounces (4 cups)
Gallon	128 ounces (4 quarts)

Bottle Sizes/Ounces

| Split/6.3 | Quart/32 |
| Fifth/25.3 | Litre/33.8. |

The Basic Bar Spirits

Bourbon

Brandy/Cognac

Canadian

Gin

Liqueurs
(See Chapter 13)

Rum
(White, Gold)

Tennessee

Scotch, Blended

Scotch, Single-Malt

Tequila

Triple Sec
(See Chapter 13)

Vermouth
(See Chapter 11)

Mixers

Club Soda	Colas
Fruit Juices	Ginger Ale
Tomato/V8 Juices	Tonic Water

Spices/Garnishes

Salt and Pepper	Cherries
Sugar	Lemons
Tabasco	Limes
Worcestershire	Nutmeg
Onions (Cocktail)	Olives (Black and Green)

10

CLASSIC DRINKS

A True Story

An obviously intoxicated fellow staggered up to the bar of New York's Astor Hotel and demanded, "Make me the perfect Manhattan."

The bartender raised both hands and, as if he were a magician, wiggled them at the drunk and said, "Shazam! You're the perfect Manhattan."

In this chapter you will find recipes for mixed drinks using scotch, Irish, and American whiskeys; gin, vodka, rum, and tequila. There are, of course, hundreds of mixed-drink recipes. These were selected because they are representative of the national origins of the spirits. Except for classics that are especially associated with a particular liquor and listed at the start of each category, they are listed alphabetically.

Scotch Recipes

ROB ROY

1½ to 2 oz. scotch
½ oz. sweet vermouth
dash orange bitters
maraschino cherry

➤ Mix in glass with ice, stir, strain into chilled cocktail glass, add garnish.

ROB ROY DRY

1½ to 2 oz. scotch
½ oz. dry vermouth
dash orange bitters (optional)
lemon peel

➤ Mix in glass with ice, stir, strain into chilled cocktail glass, add garnish.

ABERDEEN

1 oz. scotch
1 oz. orange juice
1 oz. lemon juice
½ oz. triple sec

➤ Mix in shaker with crushed ice, serve in chilled cocktail glass.

BALMORAL STIRRUP CUP

1½ oz. scotch
1 oz. Cointreau

dashes angostura bitters

➤ Mix with cracked ice in shaker or blender, strain into chilled cocktail glass.

BLACKWATCH

1½ oz. scotch
½ oz. curaçao
½ oz. brandy
lemon slice
mint sprig

➤ Pour over ice cubes in chilled cocktail glass, stir, add lemon slice and mint sprig.

BOBBY BURNS

1½ oz. scotch
½ oz. dry vermouth
½ oz. sweet vermouth
dash Benedictine

➤ Mix with cracked ice in shaker or blender, strain into chilled cocktail glass.

BRIGADOON

1 oz. scotch
1 oz. grapefruit juice
1 oz. dry vermouth

➤ Mix with cracked ice in shaker or blender, serve in chilled old-fashioned glass.

DUNDEE DRAM

1 oz. scotch
1 oz. gin
½ oz. Drambuie
1 tsp. lemon juice
lemon peel
maraschino cherry

➢ Mix all but fruit with cracked ice in shaker or blender, pour into chilled old-fashioned glass, twist lemon peel over glass and drop in, add cherry.

FLYING SCOT

1½ oz. scotch
½ oz. Peter Heering
1 tsp. dry vermouth

➢ Mix in shaker, serve in chilled old-fashioned glass.

GRETNA GREEN

½ oz. heather honey
1½ oz. scotch
1 oz. lemon juice
½ oz. green Chartreuse

➢ Mix honey with a little water, blend with scotch, lemon juice, and Chartreuse in shaker or blender with cracked ice, strain into chilled cocktail glass.

HEATHCLIFF

1 oz. scotch
1 oz. Calvados
½ oz. dry gin
1 tsp. heather honey or sugar syrup

➢ Mix in shaker with crushed ice, serve in chilled cocktail glass.
(Also known as Argyll cocktail.)

HIGHLAND

1½ oz. scotch
3 oz. milk
1 tsp. sugar
grated nutmeg

➢ Mix in shaker with crushed ice, serve in old-fashioned glass, nutmeg on top.

HOPSCOTCH

1½ oz. scotch
½ oz. sweet vermouth
several dashes orange bitters
olive

➢ Mix in shaker with crushed ice, pour into whiskey sour glass, add olive.

KNUCKLEBUSTER

1½ oz. scotch
¾ oz. Drambuie

➢ Pour both into old-fashoned glass with ice cubes, stir well.

LOCH NESS

1½ oz. scotch
1 oz. Pernod
¼ oz. sweet vermouth

➢ Mix with cracked ice in shaker or blender, serve in chilled cocktail glass.
(Look out for the famous underwater monster.)

PRINCE EDWARD

1½ oz. scotch
½ oz. Lillet
¼ oz. Drambuie
orange slice

➤ Mix in shaker with crushed ice, serve in chilled old-fashioned glass, add orange slice.

SCOTCH MIST

1¼ to 2 oz. scotch
lemon peel

➤ Fill old-fashioned glass with crushed ice, add twist of lemon peel, pour scotch over ice.

SCOTCH SANGAREE

1 tsp. heather honey
1½ oz. scotch
lemon twist
club soda
grated nutmeg

➤ Dissolve honey in a little water or club soda in double old-fashioned glass, add scotch, lemon twist, and ice cubes. Top with club soda and sprinkle of nutmeg.

SCOTCH SMASH

Heather honey or sugar syrup
6 mint leaves
2 or 3 oz. scotch
dash orange bitters
mint sprig

➤ Muddle honey or sugar syrup with mint in double old-fashioned glass, fill glass with crushed ice, add scotch, mix well. Top with bitters and mint sprig.

SCOTCH SOUR

1½ oz. scotch
½ oz. lemon juice
1 tsp. sugar syrup
orange slice
maraschino cherry

➤ Mix all but fruit in shaker with crushed ice, strain into chilled whiskey sour glass, add fruit garnishes.

SPIRIT OF SCOTLAND

2 oz. scotch
¾ oz. Drambuie
¼ oz. lemon juice

➤ Mix with cracked ice in shaker or blender, strain into a chilled cocktail glass.

Irish Recipes

IRISH COFFEE

1½ oz. Irish
hot coffee (the stronger the better)
brown sugar
cream

➤ Pour the Irish into a warm glass coffee mug (or Irish coffee glass), add coffee almost to the brim, stir in sugar, pour cream slowly into spoon held above glass so that cream dribbles into the coffee and settles on top; do not stir in.

BALLSBRIDGE BRACER

1½ oz. Irish
¾ oz. Irish Mist (see p. 63)
3 oz. orange juice
1 egg white

➤ Mix with cracked ice in shaker or blender, strain into chilled cocktail glass. (Makes two drinks.)

BALLYLICKEY BELT

½ tsp. heather honey or sugar syrup
1½ oz. Irish
cold club soda
lemon peel

➤ Mix honey with a little water or soda in cocktail glass, add Irish and ice cubes, top off with club soda. Twist lemon peel over and drop in.

BLACKTHORN

1½ oz. Irish
1½ oz. dry vermouth
dashes Pernod
dashes angostura bitters

➤ Mix with cracked ice in shaker or blender, serve in chilled old-fashioned glass.

CELTIC BULL

1½ oz. Irish
2 oz. beef consommé or bouillon
2 oz. tomato juice
dashes Worcestershire sauce
dash Tabasco sauce
freshly ground pepper

➤ Mix with cracked ice in shaker or blender, serve in chilled old-fashioned glass.

CORK COMFORT

1½ oz. Irish
¾ oz. sweet vermouth
dashes angostura bitters
several dashes of Southern Comfort

➤ Mix with cracked ice in shaker or blender, serve in chilled old-fashioned glass.

FOUR–LEAF CLOVER

1½ oz. Irish
1½ oz. green crème de menthe
1 oz. heavy cream
maraschino cherry

➤ Mix all but cherry in shaker with crushed ice, pour into old-fashioned glass, add cherry.

GREEN–EYED MONSTER

1¼ oz. Irish
1 oz. sweet vermouth
¼ oz. green crème de menthe
dash bitters

➤ Stir all ingredients in mixing glass, pour into chilled cocktail glass.

IRISH FIX

1 oz. Irish
½ oz. Irish Mist (see p. 63)
½ oz. lemon juice
½ oz. pineapple juice

orange slice
lemon slice

➤ Mix all but slices in blender with crushed ice, serve in old-fashioned glass, add slices.

IRISH KILT

2 oz. Irish
1 oz. scotch
1 oz. lemon juice
1½ oz. sugar syrup
dashes orange bitters

➤ Mix in shaker with crushed ice, strain into chilled cocktail glass.

IRISH SHILLELAGH

1½ oz. Irish
½ oz. sloe gin
½ oz. light rum
1 oz. lemon juice
1 tsp. sugar syrup
2 diced peach slices
5 or 6 raspberries
1 maraschino cherry

➤ Mix all but fruit in blender with crushed ice, serve in chilled old-fashioned glass, garnish with berries and cherry.
(Also known as a Leprechaun.)

PADDY COCKTAIL

1½ oz. Irish
¾ oz. sweet vermouth
dashes of bitters

➤ Mix in shaker with crushed ice, serve in chilled cocktail glass.

SHAMROCK No. 1

1½ oz. Irish
¾ oz. dry vermouth
1 tsp. green Chartreuse
1 tsp. green crème de menthe

➤ Stir with lots of ice in pitcher, strain into cocktail glass.

SHAMROCK No. 2

1½ oz. Irish
1½ oz. green crème de menthe
2 oz. heavy cream
maraschino cherry

➤ Mix with cracked ice in shaker or blender, serve in chilled old-fashioned glass, add cherry.

SHAMROCK No. 3

1½ oz. Irish
¾ oz. green crème de menthe
4 oz. vanilla ice cream

➤ Mix in blender until smooth, serve in chilled wine glass.

TIPPERARY

1 oz. Irish
1 oz. sweet vermouth
½ oz. green Chartreuse

➤ Mix in mixing glass with ice cubes, stir well, strain into chilled cocktail glass.

WARM CREAMY BUSH

½ oz. warm coffee
¾ oz. Bailey's Irish Cream
¾ oz. Bushmills

➤ Serve in shot glass.

Bourbon Recipes

ANCHORS AWAY

1 oz. bourbon
2 tsp. triple sec
2 tsp. peach brandy
2 tsp. maraschino liqueur
2 tbsp. heavy cream
several drops maraschino cherry juice

➤ Mix with cracked ice in shaker or blender, serve in chilled old-fashioned glass.

OLD FASHIONED

$1\frac{1}{2}$ to 2 oz. bourbon (also made with blended whiskey, Canadian, or rye)
dash water
dash sugar syrup
dash or 2 angostura bitters

➤ Mix in old-fashioned glass, add ice cubes.

ALLEGHENY

1 oz. bourbon
1 oz. dry vermouth
$\frac{1}{4}$ oz. blackberry brandy
$\frac{1}{4}$ oz. lemon juice
dash bitters
lemon twist

➤ Stir with ice in mixing glass, serve in cocktail glass with twist.

BEEF AND BOURBON

$1\frac{1}{2}$ oz. bourbon
4 oz. beef consommé or bouillon
juice of $\frac{1}{2}$ lemon
dashes Worcestershire sauce
1 pinch celery seed or celery salt
cucumber sticks (optional)

➤ Stir with ice in double old-fashioned glass, add cucumber.

BLIZZARD

3 oz. bourbon
1 oz. cranberry juice
1 tbsp. lemon juice
2 tbsp. sugar syrup

➤ Mix with cracked ice in shaker or blender until frosty, serve in old-fashioned glass.

BOURBON COOLER

3 oz. bourbon
$\frac{1}{2}$ oz. grenadine
1 tsp. sugar syrup
dashes peppermint schnapps
dashes orange bitters
club soda
pineapple stick

➤ Mix all but soda and pineapple with cracked ice in shaker or blender, pour into chilled tall collins glass, fill with soda, garnish.

BOURBON SIDECAR

$1\frac{1}{2}$ oz. bourbon
$\frac{3}{4}$ oz. curaçao or triple sec
$\frac{1}{2}$ oz. lemon juice

➤ Mix with cracked ice in shaker or blender, strain into chilled cocktail glass.

BOURBON SOUR

2 oz. bourbon
juice of $\frac{1}{2}$ lemon
$\frac{1}{2}$ tsp. sugar
orange slice

➤ Mix in shaker or blender with cracked ice, strain into a chilled whiskey sour glass, garnish with orange slice.

CHURCHILL DOWNS COOLER

$1\frac{1}{2}$ oz. bourbon
1 oz. brandy
2 tsp. triple sec
4 oz. ginger ale

➤ Mix all but ginger ale with cracked ice in chilled highball glass, top off with ginger ale.

DRY MAHONEY

$2\frac{1}{2}$ oz. bourbon
$\frac{1}{2}$ oz. dry vermouth
lemon peel

➤ Twist lemon peel over drink and drop in rind. (A New York version of the dry Manhattan.)

FRENCH TWIST

$1\frac{1}{2}$ oz. bourbon
$1\frac{1}{2}$ oz. brandy
$\frac{1}{2}$ oz. Grand Marnier
1 tsp. lemon juice

➤ Mix with cracked ice in shaker or blender, strain into chilled cocktail glass.

ITALIAN STALLION

$1\frac{1}{2}$ oz. bourbon
$\frac{1}{2}$ oz. Campari
$\frac{1}{2}$ oz. sweet vermouth
dash angostura bitters
lemon peel

➤ Stir with ice in pitcher, strain into chilled cocktail glass, twist lemon peel over and drop in.

LITTLE COLONEL

2 oz. bourbon
1 oz. Southern Comfort
1 oz. lime juice

➤ Mix with cracked ice in shaker or blender, strain into chilled cocktail glass.

LOUISVILLE STINGER

1 oz. bourbon
1 oz. light rum
2 tsp. white crème de cacao
2 tsp. white crème de menthe

➤ Mix with cracked ice in shaker or blender, serve in chilled cocktail glass.

MAN O' WAR

2 oz. bourbon
1 oz. orange curaçao
$\frac{1}{2}$ oz. sweet vermouth
juice of $\frac{1}{2}$ lime

➤ Mix with cracked ice in shaker or blender, serve in chilled cocktail glass.

PRESBYTERIAN

2 or 3 oz. bourbon

ginger ale
club soda

➤ Pour bourbon into chilled highball glass, add ice cubes, fill with equal parts ginger ale and soda.

RED ROVER

1½ oz. bourbon
½ oz. sloe gin
½ oz. lemon juice
1 tsp. sugar syrup
lemon slice
peach slice (optional)

➤ Mix in shaker or blender with cracked ice, strain into chilled cocktail glass, garnish.

SAZERAC

1 sugar cube
2 dashes Peychaud's bitters
dash angostura bitters
2 oz. straight bourbon (can be made with rye or blended whiskey)
dash Pernod or Herbisant
maraschino cherry

➤ Chill two old-fashioned glasses with crushed ice. Remove ice from one glass and replace it with a little water and sugar cube. Add bitters and crush sugar cube until dissolved. Add bourbon and ice cubes, stir well.

➤ Remove ice from second glass, add Pernod or Herbisant and coat inside of glass. Pour out excess.

➤ Pour contents of first glass into second, twist lemon peel over drink but do not add.

S.S. MANHATTAN

1½ oz. bourbon
½ oz. Benedictine
2 oz. orange juice

➤ Mix with cracked ice in shaker or blender, serve in chilled cocktail glass.

SWEET AND SOUR

1½ oz. bourbon
4 oz. orange juice
1 or 2 pinches sugar
pinch salt
maraschino cherry

➤ Mix in shaker or blender with cracked ice, serve in whiskey sour glass, garnish with cherry.

WALDORF COCKTAIL

1½ oz. bourbon
¾ oz. Pernod
½ oz. sweet vermouth
dash angostura bitters

➤ Stir with ice and strain into chilled cocktail glass.

WALLY WALLBANGER

1 oz. bourbon
½ oz. Galliano
1 oz. lemon juice
1 tsp. sugar syrup
sprig of mint (optional)

➤   Mix with crushed ice in shaker or blender, serve in chilled old-fashioned glass, garnish with mint sprig.

Author's favorite bourbon recipe:
PAINLESS PAUL

1½ oz. bourbon
½ oz. apricot liqueur
1 oz. grapefruit juice
1 tsp. lemon juice
dashes bitters

➤   Shake with crushed ice, serve in old-fashioned glass.

Blended Whiskey Recipes

BOILERMAKER

1½ oz. blended
12-oz. mug beer

➤   Drink whiskey straight, with beer as chaser.

OLD–FASHIONED MANHATTAN

1½ oz. blended
1½ oz. sweet vermouth
maraschino cherry

➤   Mix with cracked ice in shaker or blender, strain into chilled cocktail glass.

(Note: There are many variations on the Manhattan, depending on the addition of various bitters and other ingredients such as Dubonnet rouge, kirschwasser, Peter Heering, and liqueurs.)

AUNT GRACE'S PACIFIER

2 oz. blended
1 oz. raspberry syrup
club soda

➤   Pour whiskey and syrup into chilled old-fashioned glass, stir, add ice cubes, and top off with club soda.

DANNY'S DOWNFALL

1 oz. blended
1 oz. gin
1 oz. sweet vermouth

➤   Stir in mixing glass with ice cubes, strain into chilled cocktail glass.

GLOOM LIFTER

1½ oz. blended
¾ oz. brandy
½ oz. raspberry liqueur
1 tsp. sugar syrup
1 tsp. lemon juice
½ egg white

➤   Mix with cracked ice in shaker or blender, strain into chilled old-fashioned glass.

HORSE'S NECK

1 lemon
2 or 3 oz. blended
ginger ale

Label from Old Charter bourbon, 1937.
Courtesy United Distillers Archive, Stitzler-Weller Collection, Old Charter files

A vintage bottle, circa 1915, of Old Fitzgerald carries the label of "Bottled in Bond," referring to the government quality-control act.
Courtesy United Distillers Archive, Stitzler-Weller Collection, Old Fitzgerald files

Though the most famous of the Jack Daniel's labels is the black-and-white "Old No. 7," the label has gone through changes over the years.
Courtesy Jack Daniel Distillery

Label from Gran Centenario tequila. "100% blue agave" denotes that it is authentic tequila.

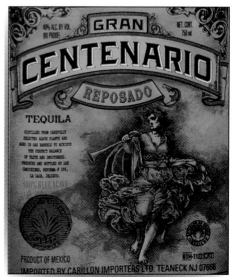

Courtesy Carillon Importers

The elegance and sophistication of a fine scotch
is reflected in this White Horse advertisement,
circa 1952.
Courtesy New York Public Library

Don Q rum was first introduced to the
United States in 1937 as seen in this
advertisement. Today, it is one of the
top-selling rums in the United States.
Courtesy New York Public Library

Cognac enjoys a reputation of worldly refinement.
Courtesy New York Public Library

The name Armagnac can only be used for
brandy made in the Gascony region of France.
Courtesy New York Public Library

The SEAGRAM'S GIN
Naked Martini.
Forget the vermouth. Just pour the perfect martini gin over the rocks.

Courtesy New York Public Library

Many advertising campaigns have included humor, such as this one for gin and the Crown Royal ad below.

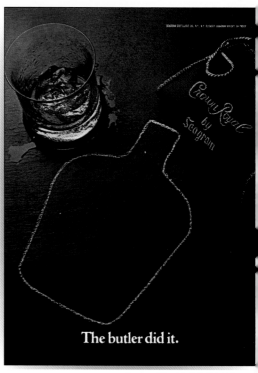

The butler did it.

Courtesy New York Public Library

Old bottles are among the prized spirits collectibles. Here is a James E. Pepper pint, circa 1930.
Courtesy United Distillers Archive, Schenley Collection, James E. Pepper files

A much sought-
after item among
collectors is this
1955 decanter from
I. W. Harper in the
form of its trademark,
Bowing Man.
Courtesy United Distillers Archive,
Bernheim Collection,
I. W. Harper files

An ad from 1956 shows "a new idea" in the form
of a pocket flask, perfect for the traveling man
who just couldn't leave home without it.
Courtesy United Distillers Archive, Bernheim Collection,
I. W. Harper files

Special-reserve whiskey is also collected by connoisseurs.
Courtesy Blanton Distilling Co.

The Bushmills
Distillery is the
oldest licensed
distillery in the
world.
*Courtesy Irish
Distillers Limited*

Scotch and Irish
whiskey were
traditionally
matured in casks
that had been
formerly used
for aging sherry.
Bushmills
continues this
practice in
making its
whiskey today.
*Courtesy Irish
Distillers Limited*

The Cascade
Distillery, circa
1890, after it was
taken over by
George A. Dickel.
*Courtesy United
Distillers Archive,
Schenley Collection,
George A. Dickel files*

Specialty brands
are often bottled
by hand.
*Courtesy Blanton
Distilling Co.*

Whiskey is prepared
for aging in white oak
barrels, which is the
American tradition of
maturing whiskey.
Courtesy Heaven Hill

The long tradition of monks as distillers has been seen world-wide. Here the story of La Grande Chartreuse, the flavorful liqueur, is recounted from its creation in the early 1600s.

Courtesy New York Public Library

Flavored liquors range from gin, flavored with juniper ...

Courtesy Shiefflein and Somerset Co.

... to Stolichnaya's series of flavored vodkas.

Courtesy Carillon Importers

➤ Peel lemon in continuous strip and put it into chilled collins glass. Add whiskey and ice cubes. Squeeze in a few drops of lemon juice. Fill with ginger ale. Stir.

MANHATTAN

1½ to 2 oz. blended
¼ to ½ oz. sweet vermouth
dash angostura bitters
maraschino cherry

➤ Mix in mixing glass or pitcher with plenty of ice, strain into chilled cocktail glass.

NEW YORKER

1½ oz. blended
½ oz. lime juice
1 tsp. sugar syrup
dash grenadine
lemon and orange peels

➤ Mix with cracked ice in shaker or blender, strain into chilled cocktail glass, twist lemon and orange peels over and drop in.

OH, HENRY!

1½ oz. blended
¼ oz. Benedictine
3 oz. ginger ale
lemon wedge

➤ Stir in chilled old-fasioned glass with ice, add lemon.

RATTLESNAKE

1½ oz. blended
1 tsp. lemon juice
1 tsp. sugar syrup
½ egg white
dashes Pernod

➤ Mix with cracked ice in shaker or blender, pour into chilled old-fashioned glass.

RED VELVET SWING

1½ oz. blended
½ oz. sloe gin
1 tsp. lemon juice
2 tsp. confectioner's sugar

➤ Mix with cracked ice in shaker or blender, strain into chilled cocktail glass.

SEVEN AND SEVEN (7&7)

1½ oz. Seagram's 7-Crown
4 oz. 7UP soda

➤ Pour 7-Crown into chilled highball glass with ice cubes, add 7UP, stir.

SUNSET GUN (SERVES 2)

4 oz. blended, rye, or bourbon
6 cloves
1 oz. curaçao
dashes orange bitters

➤ Pour whiskey in glass, add cloves. Cover and let stand for 1 hour. Remove cloves and pour into shaker or blender with cracked ice. Add curaçao and mix well. Strain into chilled cocktail glasses. Top with bitters. Add cloves.

(The name comes from the military ceremony of retreat, when a gun is fired at sundown as the flag is lowered.)

WATERLOO

1½ oz. blended
¾ oz. Mandarine Napoleon
1 tsp. lemon juice
1 tsp. sugar syrup
club soda
orange slice

➤ Mix all but soda and orange slice with cracked ice in shaker or blender, strain into chilled old-fashioned glass, top with soda, and decorate with slice.

(Because there were no blended whiskeys available when Lord Wellington won the Battle of Waterloo, the drink takes its name from the ingredient named for the loser—Napoleon.)

ZAGREB COCKTAIL

2 oz. blended
½ oz. slivovitz
1 tsp. lemon juice
1 tsp. sugar syrup
club soda
pineapple stick

➤ Mix all but soda and pineapple with cracked ice in shaker or blender, strain into chilled wine glass, top off with soda, decorate with pineapple.

Canadian Recipes

BENT NAIL

1½ oz. Canadian
½ oz. Drambuie
1 tsp. kirsch

➤ Mix with cracked ice in shaker or blender, pour into chilled cocktail glass.

CANADIAN COCKTAIL

1½ oz. Canadian
½ oz. curaçao
½ oz. lemon juice
1 tsp. sugar syrup
dash angostura bitters

➤ Mix with cracked ice in shaker or blender, pour into chilled old-fashioned glass.

CANADIAN DOG'S NOSE

2 oz. Canadian
4 oz. chilled tomato juice
1 tsp. Worcestershire sauce
½ tsp. Tabasco sauce
6 oz. cold beer
freshly ground pepper and salt

➤ Mix all but beer and salt and pepper in shaker with ice cubes, stir well. Pour into chilled collins glass. Add beer while stirring slowly. Sprinkle with salt and pepper.

CANADIAN MANHATTAN

Basic Manhattan recipe, but with Canadian whiskey.

Canadian Old-Fashioned

Basic old-fashioned with Canadian whiskey.

Dog Sled

2 oz. Canadian
2 oz. orange juice
1 tbsp. lemon juice
1 tsp. grenadine

➤ Mix with cracked ice in shaker or blender, strain into chilled old-fashioned glass.

Mammamattawa

1½ oz. Canadian
½ oz. Drambuie
¼ oz. cherry brandy

➤ Mix with cracked ice in shaker or blender, strain into chilled cocktail glass.

Maple Leaf

1 oz. Canadian
¼ oz. lemon juice
1 tsp. maple syrup

➤ Mix with ice in shaker or blender, strain into chilled cocktail glass.

Saskatoon Stinger

2 oz. Canadian
1 oz. peppermint schnapps or white crème de menthe
lemon peel

➤ Pour Canadian and schnapps into old-fashioned glass with ice cubes and gently stir, twist lemon peel and drop in.

Rye Recipes

Rye Manhattan

Basic Manhattan recipe but with rye.

Fancy Free

lemon juice
confectioner's sugar
1½ oz. rye
2 dashes maraschino liqueur
dash orange bitters
dash angostura bitters

➤ Moisten rim of cocktail glass with lemon juice. Press the glass rim into sugar. Mix rye with liqueur and bitters in shaker with cracked ice, strain into glass.

Hunter's Cocktail

1½ oz. rye
½ oz. cherry brandy
maraschino cherry

➤ Stir well in old-fasioned glass with ice, add cherry.

Lafayette

1½ oz. rye
¼ oz. dry vermouth
¼ oz. Dubonnet rouge
dashes angostura bitters

➤ Mix with cracked ice in shaker or blender, pour into chilled old-fashioned glass.

MONTE CARLO

1½ oz. rye
½ oz. Benedictine
dashes angostura bitters

➤ Mix with cracked ice in shaker, serve in cocktail glass.

ROCK AND RYE COOLER

1 oz. Rock and Rye (a citrus liqueur)
1 oz. vodka
1 tsp. lime juice
lemon-lime soda
lime slice

➤ Mix all but the soda with cracked ice in shaker or blender, pour into chilled cocktail glass. Fill with soda, garnish with lime slice.

T.N.T.

1½ oz. rye
1½ oz. Pernod

➤ Mix with cracked ice in shaker, serve in cocktail glass.

Gin Recipes

DRY MARTINI

See Chapter 11.

GIMLET

2 oz. gin

¼ oz. fresh lime juice
lime slice

➤ Mix with crushed ice in shaker, serve in chilled old-fashioned glass with slice as garnish.

(Also made with lime peel, twisted over and dropped in.)

GIN AND TONIC

1 oz. gin
tonic water
lime wedge

➤ Pour gin into chilled collins glass with ice cubes, top off with tonic water, squeeze lime wedge over and drop in.

GIN SLING

2 to 3 oz. gin
1 oz. lemon juice
½ oz. sugar syrup
club soda or water

➤ Mix in double old-fashioned glass with crushed ice, top with soda or water.

PINK GIN

2 to 3 oz. gin
½ tsp. bitters

➤ Mix with ice cubes until chilled, strain into chilled old-fashioned glass.

(Also called Gin and Bitters.)

SINGAPORE SLING

2 oz. gin
1 oz. cherry brandy
juice of ½ lemon

dash of Benedictine
club soda
lemon slice
mint sprig (optional)

➢ Mix all but garnishes with splash of soda (or water) in shaker or blender. Strain into chilled 12-ounce collins glass. Add ice cubes, top off with club soda. Garnish.

TOM COLLINS

2 to 3 oz. gin
1½ oz. lemon juice
½ oz. sugar syrup
club soda
maraschino cherry

➢ Mix with ice in tall collins glass, top off with club soda, add cherry.

ALMOND COCKTAIL

2 oz. gin
1 oz. dry vermouth
6 slivered almonds
1 crushed peach kernel
½ tsp. sugar syrup
1 tsp. kirsch
½ oz. peach brandy

➢ Warm the gin, add vermouth, almonds, peach kernel, and syrup. Chill and pour into chilled old-fashioned glass with ice cubes. Add kirsch and brandy. Stir.

AVIATION

1½ oz. gin
½ oz. lemon juice
½ tsp. maraschino liqueur
½ tsp. apricot brandy

➢ Mix with cracked ice in shaker or blender, strain into chilled cocktail glass.

BEE'S KNEES

1½ oz. gin
1 tsp. honey
dashes lemon juice

➢ Mix with cracked ice in shaker or blender, strain into chilled cocktail glass.

BISHOP'S COCKTAIL

2 oz. gin
2 oz. ginger wine

➢ Mix with cracked ice in shaker or blender, strain into chilled cocktail glass.

BLOODHOUND

1½ oz. gin
½ oz. sweet vermouth
½ oz. dry vermouth
1 tsp. strawberry liqueur

➢ Mix with cracked ice in shaker or blender, strain into chilled cocktail glass.

BROKEN SPUR

1 oz. gin
1½ oz. white port
1 oz. sweet vermouth
1 tsp. anisette
1 egg yolk

➢ Mix with cracked ice in shaker or blender, pour into chilled old-fashioned glass.

BRONX COCKTAIL

1½ oz. gin
½ oz. orange juice
dash dry vermouth
dash sweet vermouth

➤   Mix with cracked ice in shaker or blender, strain into chilled cocktail glass.

(To make a dry Bronx cocktail, omit the sweet vermouth.)

BULLDOG CAFE

½ oz. gin
½ oz. rye
½ oz. sweet vermouth
½ oz. brandy

➤   Mix with cracked ice in shaker or blender, strain into chilled cocktail glass.

CLOVER CLUB

1½ oz. gin
1 oz. lime juice
½ oz. grenadine
½ egg white

➤   Mix with cracked ice in shaker or blender, strain into chilled cocktail glass.

COLONY CLUB

1½ oz. gin
1 tsp. anisette
dashes orange bitters

➤   Mix with cracked ice in shaker or blender, strain into chilled cocktail glass.

DAMN THE WEATHER

1½ oz. gin

¾ oz. Peter Heering
¼ oz. kirsch
½ oz. lime juice
½ oz. sugar syrup
club soda
lime slice

➤   Mix with cracked ice in shaker or blender, strain into chilled collins glass, fill with soda, garnish.

DOUGLAS FAIRBANKS

2 oz. gin
¾ oz. apricot brandy
1 oz. lemon juice
1 tsp. sugar syrup
½ egg white

➤   Mix with cracked ice in shaker or blender, strain into chilled cocktail glass.

(Warning: You may feel the urge to leap around rooftops and challenge others to duels with swords.)

GIN FIZZ

2 to 3 oz. gin
½ oz. sugar syrup
juice ½ lemon
juice ½ lime
club soda
maracschino cherry

➤   Mix in shaker or blender, pour into chilled highball glass, fill with club soda, add cherry.

JUPITER COCKTAIL

1½ oz. gin
¾ oz. French vermouth

1 tsp. parfait amour or crème de violette
dashes lemon juice
1 tsp. orange juice

➤ Mix with cracked ice in shaker or blender, strain into chilled cocktail glass.

LITTLE DEVIL

1 oz. gin
1 oz. gold rum
½ oz. triple sec
½ oz. lemon juice

➤ Mix with cracked ice, strain into chilled cocktail glass.

MERRY WIDOW

1 oz. gin
1 oz. dry vermouth
dashes Pernod
dashes Benedictine
dashes Peychaud's
lemon peel

➤ Mix with cracked ice in shaker or blender, strain into chilled cocktail glass, twist lemon peel and drop in.

MISSISSIPPI MULE

1½ oz. gin
¼ oz. crème de cassis
¼ oz. lemon juice

➤ Mix with cracked ice in shaker or blender, pour into chilled old-fashioned glass.

MULE'S HIND LEG

¾ oz. gin

¾ oz. apple brandy
¾ oz. Benedictine
¾ oz. apricot brandy
¾ oz. maple syrup

➤ Mix with cracked ice in shaker or blender, strain into chilled cocktail glass.

NORMANDY

1½ oz. gin
¾ oz. Calvados or applejack
½ oz. apricot brandy
dashes lemon juice

➤ Mix with cracked ice in shaker or blender, strain into chilled cocktail glass.

ORANGE BLOSSOM

1½ oz. gin
1 oz. orange juice
orange slice

➤ Mix with cracked ice in shaker or blender, strain into chilled cocktail glass, decorate with slice.

RED LION

1 oz. gin
1 oz. Grand Marnier
½ oz. orange juice
½ oz. lemon juice

➤ Mix with cracked ice in shaker or blender, strain into chilled cocktail glass.

WHITE CARGO

1½ oz. gin
½ oz. maraschino liqueur
dash dry white wine

scoop vanilla ice cream

➤ Mix in blender until smooth, serve in chilled wine glass.

ZAMBOANGA HUMMER

½ oz. gin
½ oz. gold rum
½ oz. brandy
½ oz. curaçao or triple sec
2 oz. orange juice
2 oz. pineapple juice
½ oz. lemon juice
1 tsp. brown sugar

➤ Fill mixing glass with 3 ounces ice, add all ingredients, shake well, strain into iced-filled collins glass.

ZANZIBAR

1 oz. gin
2½ oz. dry vermouth
½ oz. lemon juice
1 tsp. sugar syrup
2 or 3 dashes orange bitters
lemon twist

➤ Fill mixing glass with ice, add ingredients and shake, strain into chilled sour glass, garnish with lemon twist.

Vodka Recipes

BLOODY MARY

2 oz. vodka
4 to 6 oz. tomato juice
1 tsp. lemon juice
¼ tsp. Worcestershire sauce
dashes Tabasco

pinch white pepper
pinches celery salt
½ tsp. chopped dill

➤ Mix with cracked ice in shaker or blender, strain into chilled collins glass, add ice cubes.

SCREWDRIVER

1½ oz. vodka
4 oz. orange juice
orange slice

➤ Pour vodka and orange juice into chilled double old-fashioned glass filled with ice cubes, stir, garnish with slice.

BLACK RUSSIAN

1½ oz. vodka
¾ oz. coffee liqueur

➤ Mix with cracked ice in shaker or blender, pour into chilled old-fashioned glass.

BOMBAY MARY

1½ oz. vodka
4 oz. tomato juice
½ tsp. curry powder
pinch ground coriander
pinch celery seed or salt
dash soy sauce
dash Worcestershire sauce
dash Tabasco
dash lemon juice

➤ Stir in 14-ounce double old-fashioned glass with crushed ice.

BULL SHOT

1½ to 2 oz. vodka
4 oz. beef consommé or beef bouillon
1 tsp. lemon juice
dashes Worcestershire sauce
dash Tabasco sauce
½ tsp. horseradish
pinch celery salt or seed

➤ Mix with ice cubes in chilled old-fashioned glass.

COFFEE COOLER

1½ oz. vodka
1 oz. Kahlúa
1 oz. heavy cream
4 oz. iced coffee
1 scoop coffee ice cream

➤ Mix all but ice cream with cracked ice in shaker or blender, pour into chilled double old-fashioned glass, top with ice cream.

COUNT STROGANOFF

1½ oz. vodka
¾ oz. white crème de cacao
½ oz. lemon juice

➤ Mix with cracked ice in shaker or blender, strain into chilled cocktail glass.

HARVEY WALLBANGER

1½ oz. vodka
4 oz. orange juice
½ oz. Galliano

➤ Pour vodka and orange juice into chilled collins glass with ice cubes, stir well, top with Galliano.

MOSCOW MULE

2 or 3 oz. vodka
1 tsp. lime juice
ginger beer
lime slice or wedge

➤ Pour vodka and lime juice into chilled highball glass, add ice cubes, top off with ginger beer, garnish with lime.

(This is the drink that introduced post–World War II America to vodka.)

RUSSIAN BEAR

1 oz. vodka
1 oz. dark crème de cacao
1 oz. heavy cream

➤ Mix in shaker with crushed ice, strain into chilled cocktail glass.

TOVARICH

1½ oz. vodka
¾ oz. kummel
1 tbsp. lime juice

➤ Fill mixing glass with ice, add ingredients, shake, strain into chilled cocktail glass.

VODKA GRASSHOPPER

½ oz. vodka
¾ oz. green crème de menthe
¾ oz. white crème de cacao

➤ Stir vodka and crèmes in shaker with ice, strain into chilled cocktail glass.

VODKA MARTINI

See Chapter 11.

VODKA STINGER

1½ oz. vodka
1 oz. white crème de menthe

➤ Stir vodka and crème de menthe in mixing glass with ice cubes, strain into chilled cocktail glass.

WHITE RUSSIAN

1½ oz. vodka
1 oz. white crème de cacao
¾ oz. heavy cream

➤ Mix in shaker with crushed ice, strain into chilled cocktail glass.

Rum Recipes

BACARDI COCKTAIL

3 oz. light rum
juice of ½ lime
2 dashes grenadine

➤ Combine in shaker with crushed ice and shake until frothy, serve in cocktail glass.

BETWEEN THE SHEETS

¾ oz. light rum
¾ oz. brandy
¾ oz. triple sec
¾ oz. lemon juice

➤ Mix in shaker with ice cubes, shake well, serve in chilled cocktail glass.

CUBA LIBRE

1¾ oz. light rum
Coca-Cola (or your choice of cola)
¼ lime

➤ Mix rum and cola in highball glass with ice cubes, squeeze lime over (do not drop in), stir.

(Also known as Rum and Coca-Cola.)

CUBAN DRY MANHATTAN

1½ oz. light rum
¾ oz. dry vermouth
dash bitters
twist of lemon

➤ Mix in mixing glass, strain into chilled cocktail glass, add twist.

ERNEST HEMINGWAY

1½ oz. light rum
juice of ½ lime
¼ oz. grapefruit juice
¼ oz. maraschino liqueur

➤ Mix in shaker with crushed ice, serve in chilled cocktail glass.

FROZEN DAIQUIRI

1¾ oz. light rum
juice of ½ lime
2 tsp. sugar
fruit (optional)

➤ Mix in blender with crushed ice, pour into cocktail or champagne glass.

GILLIGAN'S ISLAND

1½ oz. light rum
juice of ½ lime
¼ oz. grapefruit juice
¼ oz. maraschino liqueur

➤ Mix in shaker with crushed ice, serve in chilled cocktail glass.

MAI TAI

1 oz. Jamaican rum
1 oz. Martinique rum
½ oz. curaçao
¼ oz. rock-candy syrup
1 oz. orgeat
lime peel
mint sprig
slice of fresh pineapple

➤ Mix all but lime, mint, and pineapple with cracked ice in shaker or blender, pour into double old-fashioned glass, garnish.

PIÑA COLADA (SERVES 6)

⅔ cup light or dark rum
½ cup coconut cream
1 cup chilled pineapple juice
2 cups crushed ice
slices of pineapple on toothpicks with maraschino cherry on end

➤ Blend all but fruit at high speed for 30 seconds in electric blender. Strain into chilled cocktail glasses. Garnish.

PLANTER'S PUNCH

1½ oz. gold rum
¾ oz. bourbon

¾ oz. cognac
½ oz. sugar syrup
1 oz. lemon juice
dashes bitters
dashes Pernod
1 scoop crushed ice
club soda
1 lemon slice
1 orange slice

➤ Mix all but slices and soda with cracked ice in shaker or blender and pour into chilled highball glass. Top with soda and garnish with slices.

PUSSER'S MUD-IN-YOUR-EYE

1 oz. Pusser's rum
1 tbsp. brown sugar
¾ mug coffee
2 tbsp. powdered sugar
1 tbsp. cocoa
½ pint heavy (whipping) cream
1 tbsp. chocolate syrup

➤ Mix rum, brown sugar, and coffee in mug. Make cocoa cream topping: In a mixer, beat powdered sugar, cocoa, and cream until it stands in peaks. Top mug with cocoa cream and drizzle with chocolate syrup.

RUM COLLINS

1½ oz. light rum
1 oz. lime juice
1 oz. sugar syrup
soda water
maraschino cherry

slice of unpeeled orange on a toothpick

➤ Combine all but soda and fruit in cocktail shaker. Serve in tall collins glass. Add soda and more ice, if desired. Garnish with cherry and orange spear.

RUM OLD–FASHIONED

1¾ oz. light rum
1 sugar cube laced with 2 or 3 splashes bitters
maraschino cherry
wedge of lemon or orange
soda or water

➤ Mix rum, sugar, and cherry in old-fashioned glass, add wedge, top with soda or water.

SCORPION

1½ oz. dark rum
¾ oz. light rum
¾ oz. brandy
¼ oz. triple sec
1½ oz. orange juice
juice ½ lemon or lime
maraschino cherry

➤ Mix in shaker with crushed ice, strain into highball glass half-filled with crushed ice, drop in cherry.

TOM AND JERRY

1 egg, separated
1 tsp. confectioner's sugar
½ oz. rum
½ oz. brandy
splash of hot milk
nutmeg

➤ Beat white and yolk of egg separately. Blend in a glass. Add sugar and beat again. Stir in rum and brandy. Top with splash of milk. Sprinkle with nutmeg.

ZOMBIE

2 oz. light rum
1 oz. dark rum
½ oz. Demerara rum (151 proof)
1 oz. curaçao
1 tsp. Pernod
1 oz. lemon juice
1 oz. orange juice
1 oz. pineapppe juice
½ oz. papaya or guava juice
¼ oz. grenadine
½ oz. sugar syrup
1 strip of pineapple
mint sprig (optional)

➤ Mix all ingredients except pineapple and mint in blender, pour into chilled collins or hurricane glass, garnish with pineapple and mint.

Tequila Recipes
SANGRITA (CHASER: MAKES 14 2–OZ. SERVINGS)

2 cups tomato juice
1 cup orange juice
2 oz. lime juice
1 to 2 tsp. Tabasco
2 tsp. finely diced onion
1 to 2 tsp. Worcestershire sauce
several pinches white pepper
celery or seasoned salt to taste

➤ Mix in large pitcher with crushed ice. Strain into second pitcher and chill. Serve in shot glass as chaser.

TEQUILA SUNRISE No. 1

1½ oz. tequila
3 or 4 oz. orange juice
¾ to 1 oz. grenadine
lime slice

➤ Mix with cracked ice in shaker or blender, pour into chilled tall collins glass. Do not stir. Garnish with slice.

(This original recipe is known by sailors of the U.S. Navy as a "To-kill-ya Sunrise.")

TEQUILA SUNRISE No. 2

1½ oz. tequila
dash Cointreau or triple sec
juice of ½ lime
club soda
½ oz. crème de cassis
slice of lime
¾ to 1 oz. grenadine

➤ Mix all but grenadine and lime slice with cracked ice in shaker or blender, pour into chilled tall collins glass. Fill with soda and top with orange liqueur. Garnish with lime and gently stir. Slowly add grenadine. Do not stir.

TEQUILA SOUR

1½ oz. tequila
1 oz. lime or lemon juice
1 tsp. confectioner's sugar

➤ Mix in shaker with crushed ice, strain into chilled cocktail glass.

MARGARITA

1½ oz. tequila, white or gold
½ oz. triple sec
juice of ½ lime
coarse salt

➤ Mix tequila, triple sec, and lime juice with cracked ice in shaker or blender. Rub rim of chilled cocktail glass with piece of cut lime and coat rim of glass with salt. Strain and pour into glass and garnish with slice of lime.

BRAVE BULL

1 oz. tequila
1 oz. coffee liqueur
whipped cream

➤ Mix tequila and coffee liqueur in mixing glass with ice cubes, stir, strain into sherry glass, top with whipped cream.

COMPADRE

1 oz. tequila
⅓ oz. grenadine
4 drops maraschino liqueur
4 drops bitters

➤ Combine in shaker with crushed ice, shake hard, strain into chilled cocktail glass.

EL CID

1½ oz. tequila
1 oz. lemon or lime juice

$\frac{1}{2}$ oz. orgeat
tonic water
grenadine
lime slice

➤   Mix tequila, citrus juice, and orgeat well in tall collins glass, add crushed ice, top off with tonic water and 2 dashes grenadine, garnish with lime.

HORNY BULL

$1\frac{1}{2}$ oz. white tequila
4 to 6 oz. chilled orange juice

➤   Pour tequila into ice-filled cocktail glass, top off with orange juice, stir.

MATADOR

lime slice
coarse salt
$1\frac{1}{2}$ oz. tequila
1 oz. triple sec
1 oz. lime juice

➤   Moisten rim of cocktail glass with lime juice, press into salt. Combine ingredients with ice, strain into glass, garnish with lime.

MEXICAN RUIN

$\frac{1}{2}$ oz. tequila
$\frac{1}{2}$ oz. coffee liqueur

➤   Stir in mixing glass with crushed ice, serve in chilled cocktail glass.

MONTEZUMA

$1\frac{1}{2}$ oz. tequila
1 oz. Madeira

1 egg yolk

➤   Combine in blender with crushed ice, pour into chilled cocktail glass.

SNEAKY PETE (SERVES 2)

4 oz. tequila
1 oz. white crème de menthe
1 oz. pineapple juice
1 oz. lemon or lime juice
lime slices

➤   Mix all except fruit in shaker, strain into 2 chilled cocktail glasses, garnish with lime.

SPEEDY GONZÁLEZ

$\frac{1}{2}$ oz. tequila
3 oz. grapefruit juice
1 tsp. superfine sugar
cold club soda

➤   Mix all but soda in shaker with crushed ice, pour into tall highball glass, top with soda.

TNT (TEQUILA AND TONIC)

2 oz. tequila
$\frac{1}{2}$ oz. lime or lemon juice
6 oz. chilled tonic water
lime or lemon peel

➤   To highball glass two-thirds filled with ice cubes, add tequila and juice. Top with tonic water. Stir with lime or lemon twist.

A RECIPE IN MEMORIAM

Almost all recipes for mixed drinks have a story behind how and why they were invented and by whom. The tales of how they got their names are also interesting. Such was the case of a rum concoction invented in Hawaii by and named for Ray Thome (pronounced "TOE-MEE"). An uncle by marriage to Kevin Gordon, whose drawings adorn this book, Ray quit his job as an atomic engineer in 1960 to seek a quieter life in the sun. Settling in Kona, he landed a job as a radio disc jockey, known on the air as Tomi Tomi, and invented the drink that became popular throughout the islands.

When he was informed by his niece, Mary Benda, that his recipe would be included in this book, he was thrilled. Unfortunately, the next day, Mary received a phone call informing her that Ray had died in his sleep.

In his memory, here's his recipe for a Tomi Tomi: Mix 2 jiggers dark rum with 4 splashes Canada Dry Ginger Ale, add 1 slice lemon, squeezed.

PART IV

BEFORE AND AFTER

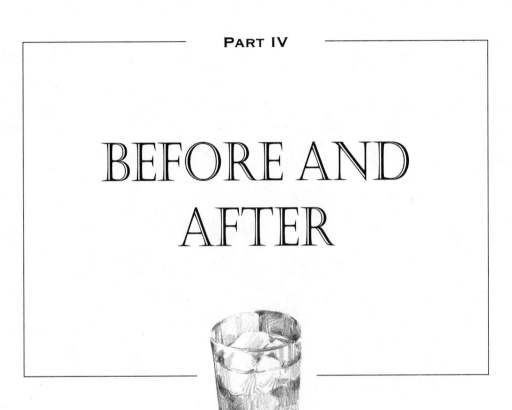

11

THE MARTINI

"The proper union of gin and vermouth is a great and sudden glory; it is one of the happiest marriages on earth and one of the shortest lived."

—BERNARD DE VOTO, 1897–1955,
The Hour

The recipe could not be simpler: a couple of ounces chilled gin, a little vermouth, drop in an olive or twist of lemon. Yet no drink evokes as much controversy and adoration among imbibers of spirits as the martini.

Must a *true* martini have an olive in it?

How much vermouth is too much vermouth?

Who needs vermouth anyway?

Shall it be mixed by stirring or shaken, à la James Bond?

Author Barnaby Conrad III holds in his book *The Martini* that 007 was right. But John Doxat, who also wrote a whole book on the martini, left no doubt from the start where he stood: He titled the volume *Stirred—Not Shaken.*

There is also a debate over the name. Was it the invention of John D. Rockefeller's bartender, Martini di Arma di Taggia, at New York's Knickerbocker Hotel in 1912? Or did it stem from the name of the Italian vermouth–making team of Martini & Rossi? The truth is, martinis were being consumed well ahead of Rockefeller and Martini & Rossi getting into the act.

We Americans had been quaffing them before the dawn of the twentieth century. One account tells about the bartender of the Occidental Hotel in San Francisco mixing one in the 1860s for a prospector en route to the gold–rush town of Martinez. There is also a claim that the drink was invented and named in that very place. Proponets of Martinez as the birthplace went so far as to put up a commemorative monument and plaque. Wherever the martini got its start, it was being mixed in 1887. A bartender's handbook of that year contained a recipe for a Martinez cocktail made of Old Tom gin, sweet vermouth, and dashes of gum syrup, bitters, and maraschino, plus a slice of lemon.

Though the recipe has varied down the years, and arguing how to make the perfect martini can still ruin a fine evening between friends or break up a romance, it has remained unquestionably an all–American favorite. It has been stirred or shaken and poured to be slowly sipped or gulped down, savored, lauded in lyrics, praised in print, immortalized in movies, and otherwise absorbed into the bloodstream of America like no other man-made drink.

The Martini Mystique

Barnaby Conrad III contended in a magazine article that the martini is distilled from the wink of a platinum blonde, a polo horse's sweat, the Chrysler Building at sunset, the smell of the aftershave of private eyes in double-breasted suits, and the blast of an ocean-liner's horn.

Food and wine authority Anthony Dias Blue, in his splendid how-to guide *The Complete Book of Mixed Drinks*, also waxed nostalgic as he wrote, "For me, the martini has always had the aura of elegance." It reminded Blue of formal dinner parties, of transatlantic crossings on the great Cunard liners, beachside cocktail parties, after-theater drinks at "21" and Fred Astaire.

If any kind of alcoholic drink came into its own in a movie, it was the martini in the hands of the dapper, sophisticated, and witty private detective Nick Charles. Created in a series of novels by Dashiell Hammett, he was brought to life on the silver screen by William Powell.

In the first of the film series, *The Thin Man*, Nick says that in making a martini by shaking it "the important thing is the rhythm." A Manhattan calls for a Bronx two-step-foxtrot time. But for a dry martini, "you always shake to waltz time."

That his wife Nora is not about to be caught flat-footed in the martini dance is proved in the next scene. Noting that Nick is six martinis ahead of her, she orders the waiter to bring her a half dozen immediately and to line them up before her.

The second most indelible martini scene on film occurs in *All About Eve*. Clutching one as she pauses on a small stairway, Bette Davis as fractious actress Margo Channing warns guests at a birthday party for her fiancé, held in her apartment, "Fasten your seat belts, it's going to be a bumpy night."

The feeling is not apprehension but frustration for Spencer Tracy in *Father of the Bride*. Having prepared a huge tray of the drink for wedding-reception guests, he discovers that everyone who enters the kitchen is interested in other drinks.

But he has no such problem in finding a partner in downing martinis in *Adam's Rib*, as costar Katharine Hepburn keeps pace with him from scene to scene. When Tracy made his last film, *Guess Who's Coming to Dinner?* Hepburn was still matching him martini to martini.

Unfortunately, Tracy did not confine his drinking to roles in movies. He was one of many Hollywood stars troubled by an inability to drink moderately, although his heavy drinking was not known generally among moviegoers.

This was not the case with one of Hollywood's open drinkers. Rarely without a drink in his hand in movies and in private life, Humphrey Bogart once complained off-screen, "The trouble with the world is that everybody in it is three drinks behind."

From Sam Spade sharing Johnnie Walker scotch with the fat man in *The Maltese Falcon* to Rick Blaine complaining that of all the gin joints in all the world the beautiful Ilsa walked into his, Bogie was a man who obviously appreciated a drink. Even his first picture with the then–eighteen–year–old Lauren Bacall was set in a French–Caribbean waterfront saloon in the screen adaptation of Ernest Hemingway's *To Have and Have Not*. Of course, few Hemingway major characters (if any) were teetotalers. Frederic Henry, World War I soldier of *A Farewell to Arms*, said a martini "made me feel civilized." Colonel Cantwell in *Across the River and into the Trees*, told a woman that he had never had a martini before meeting her.

"But you drink them very well," she replied.

So did Hemingway.

Books, plays, and poems offer what seems to be boundless references to martinis written by leading literary lights, from Jack London in 1910 to F. Scott Fitzgerald in the Roaring Twenties; Somerset Maugham, Evelyn Waugh, and Noël Coward; Dorothy Parker, Robert Benchley, and other witty scribes of the Algonquin Round Table; John O'Hara, John Dos Passos, and John Cheever; and Ian Fleming and John le Carré, the masters of fictional secret agents based on the real ones who were necessary players behind the scenes on the world stage in the aftermath of World War II.

Even before the war years, President Franklin D. Roosevelt had all but made the martini the official drink of the White House. When the cocktail hour arrived he insisted on fixing the martinis himself. The commander in chief's recipe consisted of two parts gin, one part vermouth, and a teaspoon of olive brine. Shaken. He served them at the 1943 Big Three Conference at Teheran for Winston Churchill and Joseph Stalin, neither of whom was an innocent when it came to knocking back powerful drinks.

Churchill came to the table as an old hand with martinis whose idea of adding vermouth was to glance at the bottle of it from across a room.

When FDR asked Stalin how he liked his martini, Stalin said it was "all right" but that it was "cold on the stomach." Within three years he was breaking every agreement he'd signed, thereby commencing the Cold War.

Uncle Joe's heir, the old–time Bolshevik boozer and survivor of Kremlin intrigue Nikita Khrushchev, set aside a glass of vodka to sample a martini during a summit meeting with President Kennedy. He viewed it as "America's lethal weapon."

In dealing with Khrushchev and his successors, Eisenhower, Kennedy, Johnson, Nixon, Ford, Reagan, and Bush all found reason to welcome a bracing martini from time to time and from crisis to crisis.

Of all the successors to FDR at 1600 Pennsylvania Avenue, the only one to take an official dim view of the martini was Jimmy Carter. He practically made "the three–martini lunch" a campaign issue. He complained that businessmen should not be permitted to deduct them from their taxes as costs of doing business when a laborer could not do so with the price of a bologna sandwich.

Regarding the status of the martini in the Clinton administration, Lloyd Grove of the *Washington Post* noted, "It's martini genocide at the White House. Most of the Clintonites drink white wine or get high on their own intellects. The only one that knows about martinis is James Carville. He's so high–strung that it takes two martinis to make him normal."

The apparent aversion to the martini by all but campaign adviser Carville reflects a period of decline in consumption of hard liquors that parallels the rise of the generation of Bill and Hillary Clinton. As noted earlier, the post–World War II baby boomers grew up to rebel

The martini glass reinvented for the 1990s.
Courtesy Carillon Importers, Inc.

against the established order in many ways, especially in turning their backs on anything they regarded as unhealthy.

Many claims have been made about the martini, but contributing to living a longer life has never been one of them. Although Humphrey Bogart died of cancer, as he lay upon his death bed he was able to crack, "I should never have given up scotch for martinis."

Suddenly in the 1990s, Bogie's drink is making a comeback. Along with the discovery by the kids of the baby boomers—generation X—of single-malt scotch and cigars, the marriage of gin and vermouth is being heralded anew.

So what is it about the martini to have made it a big deal?

The Dry Martini

In 1935 in *A Drink with Something in It*, humorist/poet Ogden Nash observed, "There is something about a martini." Pondering the source of its remarkably pleasant tingle, he mused, "It is not the vermouth. I think perhaps it's the gin."

Vodka notwithstanding, the distillation of the juniper berry is the basis of the martini.

The original recipe called for two parts gin, one part vermouth, and nothing else. It was often referred to as Gin and It.

DRYNESS

A dry martini is defined in terms of the ratio between gin and vermouth. The less of the latter, the drier, or stronger, it will be.

VERMOUTH

Vermouth is a wine-based processed beverage to which sugar, herbs, and other plant flavorings are added. A fine aperitif in its own right, vermouth is made in two forms: dry and sweet. The dry is what goes into a martini (sweet is used in other mixed drinks, such as the Manhattan). The best-known and most widely used brands are the Italian-made Martini & Rossi and Cinzano. A fresh bottle serves best. Connoisseurs do not recommend holding on to an opened bottle of vermouth more than a month.

THE EXTRA TOUCHES

Traditionalists insist on lemon. Cut a thin slice of rind, squeeze it with skin side down over the drink. Purists do not drop the peel in the drink, but most people do expect the rind immersed.

A colorful additive is a small green olive. Some fanciers like one stuffed with pimento. Michael Jackson's guidebook warns that if an olive is added, it must not be the stuffed variety.

Some aficionados recommend a dash of orange bitters or other embellishments.

THE GLASS

The traditional vessel for drinking a martini is stemmed and about six inches tall. The chalice is conical, straight-sided, and with a maximum capacity of four ounces. It should be chilled. A small hollow at the bottom will accomodate an olive.

MARTINI VARIATIONS

ON THE ROCKS   A dry martini poured over ice cubes into a chilled old-fashioned glass.

SWEET   Use sweet rather than dry vermouth.

GIBSON   Forget the olive and add one to three pearl onions.

VODKA   Make it with vodka instead of gin. Or both.

TEQUINI   Omit gin for tequila. Add both olive and lemon twist.

OTHER VARIETIES

Name	Variation/Addition
Allies	A few dashes of kummel.
Atta Boy	Half teaspoon of grenadine.
Dutch	Made with Dutch genever gin.
Fino	One quarter ounce fino sherry.
Hawaiian	Dashes of angostura bitters.
Imperial	Angostura and maraschino liqueur.
Mariner's	Leave out vermouth, substituting white-wine vinegar and bits of anchovies.
Martinez	Use Old Tom Gin, dash of bitters, two dashes maraschino liqueur, and 3 ounces dry vermouth.
Médoc	Add half ounce Cordial Médoc.

Name	Variation/Addition
Newbury	Several dashes curaçao with both orange and lemon peel.
Paisley	Add a half teaspoon scotch.
Palm Island	Quarter ounce crème de cacao.
Peggy Cocktail	Splashes of Dubonnet wine and Pernod.
Racquet Club	Dash of orange bitters.
Roll's Royce	Several dashes Benedictine.
Romana	Several dashes Campari.
Saketini	Substitute sake for vermouth.
Sicilian	Add a half ounce dry marsala.
Third Degree	Half teaspoon Pernod.
Yale	Splashes orange bitters, maraschino.

A Few Martini Quotations

Hands down, the best-known—"I must get out of these wet clothes and into a dry martini"—is most likely the coinage of a publicity man who attributed it to a client, humorist Robert Benchley. But its parentage has been credited to a Benchley buddy of the Algonquin Round Table's 1920s smart set, roly-poly, owlish Alexander Woollcott (after whom it is also said brandy Alexander was named). Others named as first to say it were actor Charles Butterworth and Mae West.

Here are a few other notable martini sayings:

"When you come down to brass tacks there's nothing to beat a dry martini." (Somerset Maugham, *The Fall of Edward Bannard.*)

"Happiness is finding two olives in your martini when you're hungry." (Johnny Carson, also wrote *Happiness Is a Dry Martini.*)

"Auntie Mame says olives take up too much room in a little glass." (Little Patrick Dennis, whipping up a batch in *Mame.*)

"I made him a third martini, but the women came and made us eat something, which spoiled a very promising evening." (Russell Baker, *New York Times*, April 28, 1979.)

"The finest of all cocktails." (Michael Jackson, author of *Bar & Cocktail Companion: The Connoisseur's Handbook.*)

"Angel's milk." W. C. Fields.

12

COGNAC AND BRANDY

"Mynheer Vandunk, though he never

was drunk,

Sipped brandy and water gaily."

—FRIEDRICH VON SCHILLER,
1759–1805

In assaying choices for after-dinner drinks, the English scholar who compiled a great eighteenth-century dictionary, Dr. Samuel Johnson, wrote, "Claret is for boys; port for men; but he who aspires to be a hero must drink brandy."

Like claret and port, brandy is a product of the grape. But it differs from wine in that making it continues beyond fermentation to distillation. The word *brandy* is derived from the word in some languages for *burn*, as in the American West, the burning of an identifying symbol into the hides of cattle is *branding*. When Dutch sailors first tasted the drink in France, they called it *brandewijn*, which means "burned wine."

The method dates to the Middle Ages and the invention of the still by alchemists motivated to find drinks with medicinal benefit. One of these experimenters in France in 1250 was Arnaud de Villeneuve, who wrote effusively of the wonders of distilled spirits in treating various maladies. This eau-de-vie ("water of life") was made from the grapes of the Charente region, which lies along France's Atlantic coast between the Pyrenees and Brittany. The area has been politically divided into seven parts. They are Grande Champagne and Petite Champagne (not to be confused with the wine called *champagne*), *Borderies, Fin Bois, Bois Ordinaires,* and *Bois Communs.* The capital city of the region has given its name to a drink described as "distilled quintessence of wine."

Cognac

You could say that cognac was born out of a mistake on the part of profit-seeking French wine makers. Eager to squeeze as much money as possible from the export of wines, sixteenth-century vintners figured that by distilling their wines they could save a lot of money on shipping costs. Once the concentrated wine got to its destination, whatever had evaporated during distillation would be replaced, thereby reconstituting the wine. They discovered that did not happen. Instead, they had a new kind of beverage.

Presently, three British entrepreneurs crossed the Channel to investigate the possibilities of going into the cognac trade. Testimony to the success of their ventures may be found in the form of their names on the companies they founded to manufacture the spirit: Hennessy, Hine, and Martell.

THE GRAPE

Although French law allows several white grapes to be used in making cognac, the major variety is Ugni Blanc, also known as St. Emilion, after the region. Because of the strong acidic nature of the grapes of the region, the wines produced were virtually

Hennessy distillery
Courtesy Schieffelin &
Somerset Co.

undrinkable. But what made bad wine turned out to be ideal for creating superb brandy in the copper–lined pot still.

DISTILLATION

After fermentation with a special locally grown yeast, the grapes are cooked over a wood fire. Distillation is done twice. The first (*brouillis*) is an impotable spirit of about 28 percent alcohol. The second (*double chauffe*) is 70 percent alcohol, and like all newly distilled spirits is colorless and extremely harsh and strong, requiring it to be aged in oak barrels.

AGING

The value in aging cognac also owes its discovery to a twist of history. With the outbreak of war on the continent (the War of the Spanish Successsion) the brandy makers who could not ship their wares left them in their barrels. Once the fighting was ended and the casks opened, the contents were found to have improved greatly in terms of taste and color as a result of having aged twelve years in the oak. But they also found that about a quarter of the contents had been lost through evaporation (they were the first to call it the angels' share), further intensifying the "burned wine" character.

Each cask of Hennessy is hand-stenciled.
Courtesy Schieffelin & Somerset Co.

As the spirits age, they become more and more mellow and pick up bouquet and color from the wood. The oak used in cognac making is Limousin or Troncais.

BLENDING AND BOTTLING

Rather than package the product themselves, the French distillers sold their cognac to blenders who put their own brand names on the bottles. They also devised a means of signifying the age of the cognac. The letters *VO* on a label meant very old, which was not old at all—between four and four and a half years; *VSOP* (very superior old pale) was aged up to ten; *XO* (extra old), also now called Napoleon, was a blend of brandies not less than five and a half years old, although most were between fifteen and twenty-five. Minimum age is now set by law at not less than two. How long a brandy is aged is up to the maker, although it reaches its peak and begins to deteriorate after seventy years. Once it is bottled, the aging stops.

DRINKING COGNAC

The preferred glass is the delicate tulip-shaped snifter with a capacity of five to six ounces, although no more than an ounce should be poured into it at a time. Gently swirling it will release the perfume, and smelling is as important to the enjoyment of cognac as drinking. While cognac can be an ingredient of mixed drinks (sidecar, stinger), it is best when taken neat.

Cognac is toasty and softly fruity with an intensely perfumed nose.

The following brands are classified as to body light, medium, or full, and are overall rated good (G), excellent (E), or superb (S).

Brand	Body	Rating
Bisquit	Medium	E
Camus	Medium	E
Courvoisier	Full	S
VS		
VSOP		
Napoleon		
Jean Danflou Fine Champagne	Medium	E
Grande Champagne Extra		
Davidoff	Medium	E
Delamain Pale and Dry	Light	G
Denis-Moune	Medium	E
A. de Fussigny	Light	S
Selection		
XO Imported		
Fine Champagne Vielle Reserve		
Très Vielle Grande Champagne		
Hennessy	Medium	S
VS		
VSOP		
XO		
Paradis		
Thomas Hine	Medium	S
Antique		
Family Reserve		
Rare and Delicate		
Triomphe		
Kelt Amiral	Medium	G
Les Quatre Vents		
Tour du Monde		
Martell	Full	E
Cordon Bleu		
Extra		
L'Or		

[Note: Advertised as "the pinnacle of greatness," priced at $1,099, its decanter is decorated in 24K gold.]

Brand	Body	Rating
Monnet	Medium	E

Monsieur de Bessiere
   VSOP
   Normandie Fine
	Medium	G

Noblege
   VS
   VSOP
   XO
	Medium	G

Otard	Medium	G

Pierre Ferrand
   Ambre
   Reserve
	Medium	G

Ragnaud-Sabourin	Medium	E

Remy Martin
   VSOP
   XO
   Louis XIII
   [Note: Priced around $1,000, promoted as "crowning jewel of all cognacs": 375 ml.]
   Napoleon
   Extra Perfection
	Medium–Full	S

Rothschild Napoleon	Medium	E
Salignac	Medium	G

Armagnac

This French brandy also derives its name from the region of southwestern France and has been made for more than five hundred years—two hundred years longer than cognac. Under a 1909 law, the name may be used only on brandy made within a specified area of the ancient province of Gascony. Only white grapes—Ugni Blanc, Colombard, and Folle Blanche—are used.

The distilling is done in the continuous process, resulting in a product of 110 proof. However, recent changes in regulations affecting production now permit double–distillation in pot stills. This step was taken to speed up the maturation process, thereby increasing the amount of product available to a growing market.

James Bond was a man of refined tastes. Here, a fine brandy and cigars.
Movie Still Archives

Aging was originally done in Monlezun oak, but as supplies became scarce Limousin and Troncais have come into use.

As with cognac, labels of Armagnac bottles employ a system of stars, letters, and names as indicators of age and quality. Most of the exports are VSOP.

Armagnac's full-bodied flavor is earthy and nutty with floral overtones and the fruity hint of prunes.

Armagnac is consumed in the same way as cognac.

Leading labels are:

Brand	Body	Rating
Marquis de Caussade	Medium	E
Chabot	Full	S
Château Lafite-Rothschild	Medium–Full	S
Château du Laubade	Medium	E
Cles de Ducs	Medium	E
Danflou	Medium	E
De Montal	Medium–Full	E

Brand	Body	Rating
Domaine Jouanda Lot 70	Medium	G
Dom d'Ognoas 1982	Medium	G
Francis Darroze Bas Réserve	Medium	E
Hor's d'Age	Medium	G
Hubert Dayton	Full	S
J. de Malliac	Light	E
Janneau	Light	E
Laberdolive	Full	S
Lapostolle	Medium	G
Larressingle	Full	E
Loubere	Medium	E
Marquis de Montesquiou	Full	S
Michel Reynaud	Full	S
Samalens	Medium–Full	E
Sempe	Full	S
Tarriquet Folle Blanche	Medium	G
Trepout	Medium	G

Calvados

Calvados is made from apple cider and produced only in the eponymous department in Normandy, France, where there have always been more apple orchards than vineyards. Aged in oak two to five years or more, it matures slowly, and is bottled between 80 and 86 proof.

Brand	Body	Rating
Bizouard	Full	S
Boulard Fine	Medium	G
Boulard Grande Fine	Medium	E
Busnel Hors d'Age	Full	S
Calvados Montgommery	Medium	G
Ducs de Normandie Vielle Réserve	Full	S
Ecusson Carte d'Or Vieux	Medium	G
Père Magliore	Full	E
La Pommeraie	Medium	G

American Brandy

Primarily made in the San Joaquin Valley of California from Thompson Seedless, Flame Tokay, and Emperor grapes in continuous stills, American (or California) brandy must be aged in oak at least two years. The result is a light, fruity drink that ranges from sweet to slightly dry, and is good for mixing.

The best-selling brands are Almaden, Aristocrat, Christian Brothers, Coronet, Korbel, Lejon, Old Mr. Boston, and Paul Masson. Other bottlers are A. R. Morrow, Asbach Uralt, Bealieu, Cardinal Mendoza, Conti Royal, Cresta Blanca, E & J, Fundador, Germain Robin, Italian Swiss Colony, Jepson, Juiles Domet, Petri, Pisco Montesierpe, Presidente, Raynal, Royal Host, Sr. Carneros Alambic, and Torres.

APPLEJACK

The American version of Calvados, applejack is a blend of neutral spirits and no less than 20 percent apple brandy (made from hard cider). It must be aged in oak at least two years. The major producer is Laird's in New Jersey. In 1964 the state legislature passed a resolution that designated applejack "the oldest distilled beverage in the United States."

Fruit Brandy

A brandy to which fruit flavoring has been added. Fruited brandies work well in mixed drinks. Pear brandy is made with the Williams or Bartlett variety. Other fruits used in brandy making are the strawberry (called fraise), raspberry (framboise), plums (mirabelle), and cherries (kirsch). They are made in France, Germany, Switzerland, Hungary, Yugoslavia, Romania, and the United States.

Grappa/Marc

Made from the skins, pulp, and other residue (pomace) of grapes that have been pressed for making wine, this type of brandy is known as grappa in Italy and marc in France. It is distilled in continuous-column stills (the modern version of the Coffey still). Generally they are not aged, although some manufacturers have instituted an aging process to make a mellower product. Grappa is also made in the United States.

Other Brandies

Grapes and other fruits have been turned into brandy in the following places: Spain (several brands), Greece (Metaxa), Germany (Asbach–Uralt), Peru (Pisco), Mexico (Presidente), and South Africa (K.W.V.). When Winston Churchill was given a taste of the latter he told South Africa's minister of justice, Jan Smuts, "It is excellent. But it is not brandy."

Cognac Drinks

ALABAZAM

2 oz. cognac
1 tbsp. curaçao
1 tsp. lemon juice
2 tsp. sugar syrup
2 dashes orange bitters

➤ Fill mixing glass with ice, add ingredients, shake, strain, serve on the rocks.

B & B

1 oz. cognac
1 oz. Benedictine

➤ Pour into brandy snifter, swirl to mix.

BETWEEN THE SHEETS

1½ oz. cognac
1 oz. light rum
¾ oz. curaçao
½ oz. lemon juice

➤ Mix with cracked ice in shaker or blender, strain into chilled cocktail glass.

CONCORDE

2 oz. cognac
2 oz. chilled pineapple juice
champagne

➤ Mix cognac and juice, stir, strain into champagne glass with ice, top off with champagne.

FRENCH GREEN DRAGON

1½ oz. cognac
1½ oz. green Chartreuse

➤ Fill mixing glass with ice, add cognac and Chartreuse, shake, strain, serve on the rocks.

INTERNATIONAL

1½ oz. cognac
1 tsp. vodka
2 tsp. anisette
2 tsp. Cointreau

➤ Fill mixing glass with ice, add ingredients, shake, serve in chilled cocktail glass.

WAGON WHEEL

1½ oz. cognac
2½ oz. Southern Comfort
1 oz. lemon juice
½ oz. grenadine

➤ Fill mixing glass with ice, add ingredients, shake, strain, serve on the rocks.

Brandy Drinks

BRANDY ALEXANDER

1½ oz. brandy
1 oz. crème de cacao
1 oz. heavy cream

➤ Mix with cracked ice in shaker or blender, strain into chilled cocktail glass.

SIDECAR

1½ oz. brandy
¾ oz. curaçao
½ oz. lemon juice

➤. Mix with cracked ice in shaker or blender. Strain into a chilled cocktail glass.

DEAUVILLE

1 oz. brandy
¾ oz. apple brandy
½ oz. Cointreau
½ oz. lemon juice

➤ Mix with cracked ice in shaker or blender, strain into chilled cocktail glass.

JACKROSE

2 oz. applejack
½ oz. lime or lemon juice
1 tsp. grenadine

➤ Mix with cracked ice in shaker or blender, strain into chilled cocktail glass.

LOUDSPEAKER

1 oz. brandy
1 oz. gin
¼ oz. Cointreau

½ oz. lemon juice

➤ Mix with cracked ice in shaker or blender, strain into chilled cocktail glass.

PRAIRIE OYSTER

1 egg
1½ oz. brandy
dashes Worcestershire sauce
dash cayenne pepper
dash Tabasco sauce
dash celery salt

➤ Seperate egg and place unbroken yolk in a Delmonico glass. Add all other ingredients and drink down in one gulp.

THE WHIP

1½ oz. brandy
¾ oz. sweet vermouth
¾ oz. dry vermouth
½ tsp. curaçao
dashes Pernod

➤ Mix with cracked ice in shaker or blender, strain into chilled cocktail glass.

WIDOW'S KISS

1 oz. applejack
1 oz. Benedictine
½ oz. yellow Chartreuse
dash angostura bitters

➤ Mix with cracked ice in shaker or blender, strain into chilled cocktail glass, optional garnish with a strawberry.

13

LIQUEURS AND ALL THE OTHERS

"Deo optimo maximo."

—BENEDICTINE PRAYER

The English translation of the Latin phrase on the preceding page is "To God most good, most great." Abbreviated as intials (DOM), the dedication appears on every bottle of liqueur made and sold by the monks of the Order of St. Benedict at Fécamp, France. The first monastery was established at Monte Casino, an Italian mountaintop that became famous (or infamous) during World War II when the United States Air Force was forced to bomb it to dislodge German forces who were blocking the American advance toward Rome. By 1944, however, Benedictine monasteries had been established over hundreds of years at places far from Italy, including Fécamp. There, in 1510, the monks manufactured a sweet, brown, herb–based alcoholic drink that spread over the globe to become what is arguably the world's best-known liqueur: Benedictine. A blend of herbs in a cognac base, it is aged four years and bottled at 40 proof.

It is one of many after–dinner drinks classified as liqueurs or cordials. This type of flavor–added spiritous drink is subdivided into two categories: *proprietary* means the recipe is a secret; *generic* liqueurs can be made by anyone from generally available recipes.

Proprietary Liqueurs

A century after the Benedictine monks created their special formula, another religious order, the Carthusians, went into the liqueur business with Chartreuse. Called "the elixir of long life" (*elixir de longue vie*), rather than "water of life," the recipe was given to the monks by one of Henry IV's captains. It is made from 130 plants and herbs and bottled at 84 to 110 proof. A version of it with a unique shade of green led to the coining of a word taken from the place where it was made: *chartreuse.*

Although the monks of Chartreuse let control of the making and selling of it pass into layman hands, they retained the secret to the formula and continue to make it at their distillery at Voiron in the Alpine foothills.

Drambuie is another in the proprietary category. It proudly asserts on its stout, round bottles that it is "Prince Charles Edward's Liqueur." The label notes that the name stems from the Gaelic *Dram Buidheach*, meaning "the drink that satisfies." It then goes on to say, "Drambuie forms a link with one of the most romantic episodes in the history of Great Britain" when Prince Charles came to Scotland in 1745 "to make his gallant but unsuccessful attempt to regain the throne of his ancestors." As reward to a man who had assisted him, a chap by the name of Mackinnon on the Isle of Skye, "Bonnie Prince Charlie" gave Mackinnon the secret recipe of his "personal liqueur." The Mackinnon family's treasure

At the Chartreuse distillery, a Carthusian brother measures the alcohol content with a hydrometer.
Courtesy New York Public Library

eventually became the Drambuie Liqueur Co. of Edinburgh, today's maker of the drink that is also called "the Isle of Skye Liqueur." It is bottled at 80 proof.

Another proprietary liqueur with a claim to history is Irish Mist, said to be a re-creation of an ancient recipe for the drink called Irish Heather wine that had been savored in Ireland before the recipe became lost following suppression of the Rebellion of 1691.

Italy also has a liqueur with a link to an historic person. It was born in the late 1800s and named Liquore Galliano after a hero of the Abyssinian War, Major Giuseppe Galliano. It has an herbal vanilla flavor and a syrupy texture. Produced at Livorno, Tuscany, it is a mixture of different distillations that stand for three months in order to marry. Alcohol is added to bring it to 40 percent alcohol. Its chief use in the United States is as the basis for the Harvey Wallbanger cocktail.

Proprietary Brands

Name	Flavor Basis	Country
Abtel	herbal	Israel
Ambrosia	caramel/herbal	Canada

Name	Flavor Basis	Country
B&B	Benedictine/cognac	France
Benedictine	herbal	France
Bronte	fruit	Britain
Chartreuse	herbal	France
Claristine	herbal	United States
Cordial Médoc	herbal/fruit	France
Cuarenta y Tres (43)	herbal	Spain
Elixir d'Anvers	cinnamon	Belgium
Escorial Green	herbal	Germany
Fior de Alpe	herbal	Italy
Galliano	herbal/vanilla	Italy
Goldwasser	citrus/caraway	Germany
Izarra	herbal	France
Jagermeister	herbal	Germany
Nassau Royale	herbal/vanilla	Bahamas
Strega	herbal/citrus	Italy
Trappistine	herbal/Armagnac	France
Tuaca	vanilla	Italy
Vielle Cure	herbal	France

Generic Liqueurs

These are liqueurs without the pedigree of romantic origins or famous names, and are made from nearly every kind of flavoring ingredient the world of plants offers, from almond–tasting apricot pits and currants to oranges and peppermint.

Leading brands are:

Name	Flavor Basis	Country
Amaretto di Saronno	almond	Italy
Chambord	black raspberry	France
Cherry Marnier	cherry, brandy	France
Cointreau	orange	France
Crème de banane	banana	United States, others
Crème de cassis	black currants	United States, France
Crème de menthe	mint	United States, others
Crème de Noyaux	almond, nutmeg	various

Name	Flavor Basis	Country
Crème de cacao	cacao, vanilla	various
Curaçao	bitter orange	various
Dettling Williams Pear	pear	Swiss
Dubonnet	aromatics	France
Frangelico	hazelnut	Italy
Grand Marnier	orange, cognac	France
Grenadine	pomegranate	France
Kahlúa	coffee	Mexico
Kummel	caraway, anise	Holland
Mandarin Napoleon	citrus	Belgium
Maraschino	Marasca cherry	United States, Italy
Midori	muskmelon	Japan
Parfait Amour	sweet citrus	France
Pernod	anise	France
Peter Heering	cherry	Denmark
Pim's Cup	various spices	England
Sabra	jaffa oranges	Israel
Sambuca	elderbush (licorice)	Italy
Sloe Gin	sloe (wild plum)	England, United States
Tia Maria	coffee	Jamaica
Triple Sec	bitter orange	various
Tuasca	herbs/vanilla	Italy

Bitters

Whoever named this classification of additives to spiritous drinks was as unromantic as he was accurate. Originally intended as medicinals, perhaps giving rise to the phrase "bitter medicine," bitters eventually became a way to spice up other drinks. Formulas for blending a wide range of botanicals (roots, seeds, bark, etc.) are as tightly protected as recipes of proprietary liqueurs and sometimes bear the names of their places of origin or those who came up with the blends.

Among the better known are:

Name	Flavor	Origin
Abbott's	various	United States
Amer Picon	bitter orange	France

Name	Flavor Basis	Country
Angostura	herbs	Trinidad
Calisay	chinchona	Spain
Campari	herbs, fruits	Italy
China-Martini	quinine	Italy
Cynar	artichoke	Italy
Fernet Branca	herbs	Italy
Gammel Dansk	herbs	Denmark
Jagermeister	herbs	Germany
Peychaud	herbs	United States
Unicum	herbs	Germany

Aquavit/Schnapps

Available commercially since 1498 in Sweden and 1555 in Denmark, this northern European "water of life" was intended to be a tonic. But again the designs of doctors turned into something not anticipated—a drink taken for the pleasure of it. Primarily the drink of Scandinavia, it is like wines and beers in that it is consumed along with food.

It is distilled from a mash of boiled potatoes and a grain malt. Flavoring is added at the end of the process. Among those used are caraway, dill, fennel seed, and aniseed. The Danes call the drink *schnapps* and produce more than half the world supply.

Schnapps are also German-made (spelled with one *p* in German) and may be called *Klarer*.

Schnapps are customarily taken very cold in a short glass.

Absinthe: the Forbidden Drink

"After the first glass of absinthe," said Oscar Wilde, "you see things as you wish they were. After the second you see them as they are not. Finally, you see things as they really are, and that is the most horrible thing in the world."

Some have called it the Green Muse. Others have likened its effect to that of powerful narcotics. Based on wormwood (*Artemisia absinthium*), it was blamed for causing madness and death in the early years of the twentieth century and has been banned in most countries of the world. The only legal version is found in Spain.

The licorice flavor of absinthe has been duplicated by the aniseed plant and is found in a wide range of liqueurs, including the national drink of Greece.

Absinthe, the forbidden drink
Courtesy New York Public Library

OUZO

Pronounced "OOO–zoh" and also known as douzico and raki, this clear aniseed–flavored drink will turn white when diluted with ice and water. It was aptly described in Berlitz's travel guide to Athens as having "a kick in it." The book then wisely advised, "Drink it in moderation and nibble something at the same time, as the Athenians do."

SAMBUCA

Similar to French and Spanish sweet anis liqueurs, sambuca is a colorless drink that gets its licorice taste from the elderbush. Its proof is 80 or more. It is often infused with coffee. The major brands are Sambuca Romana, Bucca di Amore, Galliano, Molinari, and Patrician Sarti.

Aquavit Recipes

ALLIANCE

1 oz. gin
1 oz. dry vermouth
2 dashes aquavit

➤   Shake in mixing glass, strain, serve on the rocks.

DANISH MARY

1 oz. aquavit
Bloody Mary mix:
½ oz. vodka
3 oz. tomato juice
½ oz. lemon juice
3 drops Tabasco sauce

3 drops Worcestershire sauce
pinch celery salt
pinch pepper
dab horseradish
celery stalk or lime slice

➢ Shake Bloody Mary mix well. Fill highball glass with ice, add mix and aquavit, stir, garnish.

VIKING

1 oz. aquavit
1½ oz. Swedish Punsch
1 oz. lime juice

➢ Pour ingredients into mixing glass with ice, shake, strain, serve on the rocks.

Sambuca Recipes

SLIPPERY NIPPLE

2 oz. sambuca
1½ oz. Bailey's Irish Cream
drop grenadine

➢ Pour sambuca into cocktail glass. Float Bailey's Cream on top. Put a drop of grenadine in the center.

Extra-brave souls add a shot of Kahlúa.

ASSASSINO

2 oz. whiskey
1 oz. dry vermouth
1 oz. pineapple juice
1 oz. club soda
2 or 3 dashes Sambuca Romana

➢ Fill mixing glass with ice, add all but sambuca and soda, shake. Strain into collins glass, top with soda, add ice. Sambuca goes on top.

BLACK LICORICE

½ oz. sambuca
½ oz. Kahlúa

➢ Combine in brandy snifter or pony glass.

LITTLE PURPLE MEN

1 oz. sambuca
1 oz. Chambord

➢ Combine in brandy snifter.

SHANGHAI

1 oz. sambuca
1½ oz. dark rum
½ oz. lemon juice
3 drops grenadine

➢ Fill mixing glass with ice, add ingredients, shake, strain into chilled cocktail glass.

Ouzo Recipe

GOOD AND PLENTY

¾ oz. ouzo
¾ oz. anisette

➢ Combine in brandy snifter or liqueur glass.

Ouzo

Ouzo is an especially interesting drink to accompany a meal in a sidewalk café with a view of the Parthenon perched on top of the Acropolis, or as you dine on seafood straight from the Aegean Sea at a harborside outdoor restaurant in Piraiévs where a strolling mandolin player will entertain you with "Never on Sunday," the title song of the movie starring Melina Mercouri. Ouzo will also help you summon the nerve to get up and take part in a dance that ends in the clatter of smashing dinner plates on the floor of a taverna, the Greek version of gathering places of high-spirited people throughout history and around the globe.

PART V

LAST
CALL

14

"SET 'EM UP, JOE"

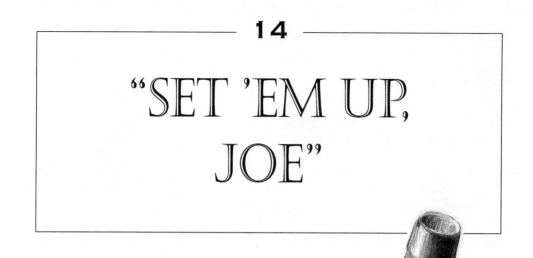

"I intend to die in a tavern . . . so that when the angels come they may say, 'God be merciful to this drinker.'"

—WALTER MAPES, 1140–1210

In the year 1609 the affable Dutch explorer Henry Hudson left his ship *Half Moon* to set foot on a New World island set in a vast harbor, and in so doing met a group of native inhabitants. Members of the Delaware tribe, they were fishing at the time. As a gesture of goodwill, Hudson gave their leader a cup of brandy. The chief got drunk. But when he woke up he asked for more, as well as a round for his tribesmen. Later, they called the island *Manahachtanienk*—translated from the Delaware language as "the high island," not in topographical meaning but as in "the island where we all got drunk."

The Delawares were not the last people to remember the isle of Manhattan that way. The city that grew upon it has earned its nickname the City That Never Sleeps in large measure because of a hospitality engendered by the many drinking emporiums that are the legacy of the people who transformed Dutch New Amsterdam into New York. In doing so they kept faith with one of England's most quotable men, Dr. Samuel Johnson, who advised, "There is nothing which has yet been conceived by man, by which so much happiness is produced, as by a good tavern or inn."

In the England of Dr. Johnson's time (1709–84) there existed plenty of them. Although hostelries for travelers had popped up along the ancient trade routes of the Orient and later beside the coach roads of Europe, it is reasonable to say that the English elevated the inn from a mere resting place for people en route from one spot to another to an establishment that also served to sate the hunger and quench the thirst of the locals: the "public house," which the English, with their penchant for shorthand (genevre=gin; rumbullion=rum; distillery=still), soon called a pub.

When Britain expanded into an empire with colonies in North America, a network of coach turnpikes that connected them called for the building of way stations. Blossoming towns and thriving new cities also demanded taverns. So appreciative of them were colonists that one law regulating the sale of spiritous drinks referred to the tavern as "one of the good creatures of God, to be received with thanksgiving." The laws required taverns not only to sell liquor but to keep sufficient quantities on hand for all happy occasions in which celebrations were in order—weddings and births, for example.

It may send shudders through health-conscious Americans at the end of the twentieth century to learn this, but at the birth of the United States of America in 1776 hard liquor was viewed as a boon to health. Rum and milk were prescribed for pregnancies. The aching gums of teething babies were rinsed with brandy. If an abstainer obtained a life insurance policy he paid a *higher* rate (10 percent more) than an imbiber.

Neither did clergymen rail against drinking spirits. At the ordination of a minister in Massachusetts in 1729, the people of Woborn picked up the bill for the new reverend's two gallons of brandy and four gallons of rum.

Benjamin Franklin, who welcomed his flagon of rum, advised, "There can't be good Living where there is not good Drinking."

Two years after the Whiskey Rebellion, the United States had a population of a little more than four million, and 2,500 registered distilleries turning out 5,200,000 gallons. Combined with imported spirits of around 11,000,000 gallons, the per capita consumption was 2.5 gallons per year. By 1810 it was up to 4.5 gallons in a populace that had barely doubled, while distilleries had multiplied to 14,191. But none of these figures included the untolled illegal stills in operation everywhere.

As the country expanded, so did the need for taverns along trails that became roads and then highways, as well as inns and hotels in the new towns—all of them offering to soothe travel-parched throats various drinks to both quench thirst and boost the spirit. Presently, entrepreneurs recognized the potential for profit, as well as public service, in opening places that sold only drinks, and not just to wayfarers. Neighborhoods soon had their own drinking salons. Americanization made them saloons.

"Just mention 'saloon,'" went a song of the 1890s, "and my cares fade away."

The institution enriched the language. In a saloon called a barrelhouse, where whiskey was dispensed from a cask, a nickel purchased a brimming shot glass. Saloons offering a free lunch found they had to post lookouts to guard against any nondrinking freeloader who might appear the minute the food was set out on the bar. Chasing away such an interloper—the beefy individual who did this was a "bouncer"—was referred to as performing the "bum's rush."

A class of these individuals proliferated along a stretch of Lower East Side Manhattan real estate whose name reflected New York's Dutch heritage. Once known as the Bouwerie (Dutch for "farm"), the Bowery of the 1890s had side-by-side saloons. These were called "distilleries" and "morgues" and peddled liquor for a nickel. On occasion a patron would be allowed all that he could guzzle through a hose connected to a barrel—without pausing for a breath. Those who patronized these places evidently did nothing else but drink and were called Bowery bums.

Some proprietors of these places got so rich they stepped up in stature by opening more genteel saloons they called clubs and cafés. Catering to high society, these men were the first of many saloon keepers whose names became part of the warp and woof of our social, political, and cultural history. At the same time they wove whiskey and other spirits tightly into that tapestry.

Among them was Steve Brodie. Operator of a Bowery saloon, he decided to get publicity for his establishment by "jumping" off the Brooklyn Bridge. Whether he did it and survived to tell of it or perpetrated a hoax has never been settled. But to this day the act of leaping from a bridge in cop terminology is "doing a Brodie."

A contemporary of Brodie, John McSorley, opened his ale house in lower Manhattan in 1854 and served drinks himself right up to his eighty-seventh year, 1910. Only the militancy of the feminist movement seven decades later could force open the doors of McSorley's Ale House to women.

Perhaps no bar is more famous or more beloved than Rick's Café Americain.   Bettman Archives

Then there was a tavern owner who was immortalized in 1899 by author Gerald Brennan, who wrote in *Shanahan's Ould Shebeen*, "If you couldn't afford good whiskey, he'd take you on trust for beer."

Perhaps the least known today but immensely significant bartenders of the nineteenth century, in terms of his legacy, was Jerry Thomas, known affectionately then as Professor. Manning the bar at the Metropolitan Hotel until 1859, he published *The Bon Vivant's Companion, or How to Mix Drinks*. It was a first of a kind. As were many of his mixed drinks, including the Blue Blazer and the Tom and Jerry. The Blazer was made with whiskey and boiling water, then set afire and poured from one glass into another for a spectacular show. The Tom and Jerry was a punch of spiced egg, sugar, and rum, mixed into a wine glass of brandy.

One of the earliest American mixed drinks was described in 1849 in a novel by Frances (Fanny) Trollope. An English woman who had hoped to become rich in the United States only to be bitterly disappointed, she returned to Britain to write a scathing indictment of American manners, especially tobacco–juice spitting. In the United States, those who agreed with her regarding the nasty practice would scold such a spitter by wagging a finger and shouting at him, "Trollope!" The epithet eventually became *trollop*, meaning a loose woman.

One thing American that did meet with Fanny's approval was the mint julep. In her novel *The Old World and the New*, Trollope called the combination of whiskey, ice, and mint leaves a beverage "that must create a delicious sensation of coolness . . . and revival of strength where strength seemed gone forever."

When Fanny's son Anthony toured the United States and wrote about the country and its people, he took a dim view of drinking habits. He wrote, "I do not intend hereby to accuse Americans of drinking too much, but I maintain that what they do drink, they drink in the most uncomfortable manner that the imagination can devise." He meant what he called getting "liquored up" at the hotel's bar at any hour of the day or evening.

In England, proper people did *not* belly up to a bar.

Of drinkers in Missouri, he wrote condemningly, "They drink, but are seldom drunk to the eye; they begin at it early in the morning, and take it in a solemn, sullen, ugly manner, standing always at a bar, swallowing their spirits, and saying nothing as they swallow it. They drink often, and to great excess."

Yet foreigners were not alone in disdaining such drinking. Many Americans regarded the word *saloon* as a synonym for *evil*. This feeling was first exhibited by enactment across the country of laws that forbade selling liquor on Sundays. Before long this prohibitionist sentiment grew powerful enough to bring about the Eighteenth Amendment to the Constitution of the United States.

Under its authority, the head of the Prohibition Unit of the Bureau of Internal Revenue, Commissioner John F. Kramer, pledged, "This law will be obeyed in cities large and small, and in villages, and where it is not obeyed it will be enforced." He also vowed that liquor would not be "manufactured nor sold nor given away nor hauled in anything on the surface of the earth or under the earth or in the air."

A pharmacy doubling as a bootlegger is found out by the authorities.
Courtesy New York Public Library

He was answered with defiance in the guises of bootleggers, rumrunners, gangsters, bathtub gin, and, because the law did not ban drinking the stuff you already had at home, the suddenly fashionable phenomenon called the cocktail party. And the speakeasy.

Out of the latter consequence of Prohibition emerged a new style of entrepreneurial capitalist who opened illegal saloons, survived the great dry spell, and went on to thrive as restaurateurs (New York's "21" being the last of the former speakeasies in existence) and impresarios of world-famous nightclubs, such as Sherman Billingsley of the Stork Club and John Perona, founder of El Morocco (also known to patrons as Elmo's).

These and other saloon operators, tavern and bar owners, and bartenders found themselves voted by grateful drinkers into the pantheon of American folk heroes in the cause of the right of an American to have a drink.

During the Depression of the 1930s, the four years of World War II, and in the immediate postwar period other names went onto the roster: Toots Shor, ex-boxing champion Jack Dempsey, Lou Walters of the Latin Quarter (the father of Barbara Walters), Hollywood's faux-Russian prince Sid Romanov, Lindy of Lindy's, and many more.

As if there were not enough real bartenders, radio offered *Duffy's Tavern*. One of the top-rated shows of the 1940s, it came on the air to the tune of "When Irish Eyes Are Smiling." Then a man answered a telephone with, "Hello, Duffy's Tavern, where the elite meet to eat. Archie, the manager, speaking. Duffy ain't here. Oh, hello, Duffy . . ." (Throughout the long run of the show on the air, Duffy never appeared.)

A decade later, television brought Jackie Gleason's Joe the bartender into living rooms, thereby blazing a trail for *Cheers* in the 1980s.

Through all these years the man behind the bar in reality and imagination grew into everyone's friend and a discreet and reliable shoulder to cry on.

In the song "One for the Road" he was the person to whom Frank Sinatra turned at a quarter to three and pleaded, "Set 'em up Joe, I've got a little story that you ought to know."

A post-Sinatra popular song that captured the mood of the modern American bar was Billy Joel's *Piano Man*, a rather glum portrait of lonely, dream-shattered drinkers written on the basis of Joel's years as a cocktail-lounge pianist.

But, has there ever been a saloon *keeper* in the history of movies more anguished than the proprietor of Rick's Café Americain in *Casablanca*? Everyone who has ever seen him on screen as he gazed at the drink before him can recite what he is about to moan: "Of all the gin joints in all the towns in all the world, she walks into mine."

Whether it's in a Rick's Café Americain somewhere, an Irish pub in Boston, a New York hotel's cocktail room, a Philadelphia tap room, a Capitol Hill bistro in Washington, a nightclub in Atlanta or Miami, a lounge at O'Hare Airport in Chicago, a saloon in Kansas City or New Orleans, a trendy bar owned by a celebrity at a Colorado or Nevada resort or along the Sunset Strip, or a bar with a particular clientele (cops, journalists, one in New York for doctors from a nearby hospital center called the Recovery Room, Wall Streeters, athletes, and you name 'em), the central figure—the maestro—is the all–knowing alchemist behind the bar.

TOASTS

No matter where you go, you'll find a uniquely nationalist flavoring to the worldwide custom of saying something before a drink goes down the hatch. The following are some of them listed by country, with translations as needed.

Australia	Cheers!	
Britain	Cheers!	
China/Japan	Kan pei!	Bottoms up.
Denmark, Iceland, Norway, Sweden	Skal!	I salute you.
Finland	Kippis!	Cheers.
France	A votre santé.	To your health.
Germany	Prosit!	Cheers. Your health.
Greece	Stin ygia sou!	Health.
Hawaii	Kamau!	Here's how.
Hungary	Egeszegedre!	Your health.
Ireland/Scotland	Slainthe.	Health. (For more Irish toasts, see below)
Israel	L'chaim!	To life.
Italy	Cin-cin!	All good things.
Mexico/Spain	Salud.	Health.
Philippines	Mabuhay!	Long life.
Poland	Na zdrowie!	Health to you.
Portugal	A sua saude!	To your health.
Romania	Noroc!	Good luck.
Russia	Za veshe z-dorovye!	Your health.
Singapore	Yam seng!	Continued success.
Yugoslavia	Zivelli!	Your health.

IRISH TOASTS/BLESSINGS

Erin go bragh! (Ireland forever!)

May you get the reward in heaven that's been denied you for your goodness on earth.

May the toes of your feet always steer you from misfortune.

Let the dust of your carriage blind your enemies.

God's fresh blessings be about you.

May the earth be soft under you when you rest upon it, tired at the end of the day, and may it rest easy over you when, at last, you lay out under it.

I wish you walls for the wind, a roof for the rain, tea beside the fire, laughter to cheer you, those who love you near you, and all that your heart might desire.

May the road rise to meet you.
May the wind be always at your back.
May the sun shine warm upon your face,
And the rains fall soft upon your fields.
And until we meet again
May God hold you in the palm of His hand.

CLASSIC TOASTS

Here's to lying, cheating, stealing, and drinking.
When you lie, lie to save a friend.
When you cheat, cheat death.
When you steal, steal a maiden's heart.
When you drink, drink with me my friend.
(courtesy, Kevin Gordon)

Here's lookin' at you, kid. (Bogart in *Casablanca*)

Mud in your eye!

Up to the lips and over the gums,
look out stomach, here it comes.

May all your troubles be little ones. (Wedding toast)

Let us wet our whistles. (Petronius)

May you live all the days of your life. (Jonathan Swift)

Down the hatch.

Here's to your enemy's enemies.

Who loves ya, baby? (Telly Savalas in *Kojak*)

Here's looking up your kilt. (Scottish)

Here's to the maiden of bashful fifteen;
Here's to the widow of fifty;
Here's to the flaunting, extravagant queen,
And here's to the housewife thrifty.
Let the toast pass–
Drink to the lass;
I'll warrant she'll prove an excuse for the glass.

> —RICHARD BRINSLEY SHERIDAN,
> *The School for Scandal, 1777*

Here's to you, as good as you are,
And here's to me, as bad as I am;
And as bad as I am, and as good as you are,
I'm as good as you are, as bad as I am. (Scottish)

Say, boys! if you give me just another whiskey
    I'll be glad,
And I'll draw right here a picture of the face
    that drove me mad.
Give me that piece of chalk with which you mark
    the baseball score,
You shall see the lovely Madeleine upon
    the barroom floor.

—Hugh Antoine D'Arcy,
    The Face upon the Barroom Floor

15

LADIES WELCOME

"What a Swell Party This Is."

—SONG TITLE,
High Society

When Oscar Wilde announced his discovery that alcohol taken in sufficient quantities produced intoxication, the wittiest man of letters of the British Empire evidently chose not to offend Victorian Age sensibilities by also pointing out that getting intoxicated was more often than not a prelude to romance.

Certainly Wilde appreciated that a collaboration of Bacchus, god of drink, with Eros, deity of love, had been a favorite theme in art, poetry, drama, music, and literature. Since the Greeks and the Romans, the muses had extolled the place of intoxicating drink in the male/female equation. Even the Book of Ecclesiastes (8:15) had advised, "A man hath no better thing under the sun, than to eat, and to drink, and to be merry." Certainly, in any Victorian interpretation of the Old Testament, being merry would have meant having sex.

The greatest of coiners of clever phrases, Anonymous, said, "Man is the only animal that eats when he is not hungry, drinks when he is not thirsty, and makes love at all seasons." And when the team of Alan Jay Lerner and Frederick Lowe included in their musical *Gigi* the giddy "The Night They Invented Champagne," they were reiterating William Sydney Porter, who writing as O. Henry in *The Gentle Grafter*, opined in 1908, "There are two times when you can never tell what is going to happen. One is when a man takes his first drink; and the other is when a woman takes her latest."

Or, as Dorothy Parker quipped poetically:

> *I like to have a martini*
> *Two at the very most—*
> *After three I'm under the table,*
> *After four I'm under my host.*

Women and Drinking

Nothing motivated the prohibitionist movement in the United States more than women, and nothing motivated the women more than their conviction that when men drank wives and children suffered.

A Puritan has been defined as "someone terribly afraid that somewhere somebody is having a good time." A prohibitionist was usually a married woman who feared that somewhere somebody's husband was about to squander his wages on whiskey and that as he bent his arm to hoist a glass there was undoubtedly a devil in the shape of a loose woman at his elbow to egg him on.

Frances E. Willard, founder of the World's Women's Christian Temperence Union (WCTU), was heralded as the Uncrowned Queen of American Womanhood and became the first woman to be honored by the Congress of the United States when it authorized a memorial to her in Statuary Hall.

In 1891 John Greenleaf Whittier wrote a poem about her:

> *She knew the power of banded ill*
> *But felt that love was stronger still,*
> *And organized for doing good,*
> *The world's united womanhood.*

As she was down on drink, so was she against tobacco. She called them "the great separatists" and wrote that "woman's evolution has carried her beyond them."

Not quite.

Cigareets, Whusky, and Wild, Wild Women

Willard's rosy portrait of the evolution of women beyond the use of tobacco and alcohol was hardly an accurate reflection of the United States—or the world, for that matter. Right up to the peak of Willard's prominence in the 1890s, American women were not only consumers but purveyors of strong drink, especially in the cities of the East Coast.

In the years before the Civil War the finest saloons in New York City hired women to entice men to drink a little more. Known to the men as "pretty waiter girls," they were nineteenth-century precursers of the 1960s' Playboy Bunnies. The writer of *Night Side of New York* looked at one of these lovelies and wrote, "As down her back fall clusters of pendent curls and as she tosses a well-shaped hand, very conscious of her winning charms, there is a queenly grace that in hearts less steeled than the major portion of the youths about town would work fearful havoc."

No wonder the ladies at home worried!

A condition laid down in the hiring of these "pretty waiter girls" stated, "it is absolutely necessary to patronize the bar."

Establishments that did not employ women instituted a policy of admitting them onto the premises as customers, signified by a sign in the window reading "Ladies Welcome."

"Out West" ladies were not just welcome in the barrooms. Some women owned them and could keep up with any man in a cow town in downing whiskeys such as Thompson's Snakehead (so called because a keg of it supposedly contained six rattlesnake heads for an extra jolt), Tarantula Juice, Forty-rod, Rookus Juice, Tanglefoot, and Taos Lightning.

A stylish group of celebrants toasts the repeal of Prohibition.
Courtesy New York Public Library

Three decades after a network of railroads eliminated the need for cattle drives and spelled doom for the raucous cow-town saloons of so many cowboy movies, a young woman from Texas hit New York City just in time for the birth of the speakeasy and nightclub. Her name was Mary Louise Cecilia Guinan, but everyone knew her as Texas.

The most lastingly famous woman in the history of drinking in America, she was a rambunctious loudmouth nightclub "hostess" who greeted anyone who forked over a cover charge just for the privilege of walking into the El Fey Club. They howled happily when she welcomed them with, "Hello suckers! Have all the laughs you can, 'cause they'll be on the bill."

When she asked one boozy customer what he did for a living, he answered, "Dairies." Texas blared, "Well, let's have a hand for the big butter-and-egg man." The phrase has stood for *big spender* in bars ever since.

Keeping up with Texas Guinan in the brashness department and also as symbols of the newly liberated women of the 1920s were singers Sophie Tucker and Mae West, whose

"Why don't you come up and see me sometime?" implied a whole lot more than prospects of getting a free drink.

According to a man who was there, Lucius Beebe, New York society in the 1920s "found itself living frankly, unabashedly, and almost entirely in saloons."

Suddenly, women who before Prohibition might cross a street rather than pass in front of a saloon were entering speakeasies and doing their drinking *at the bars*. And influencing them.

"Gone were the days when a popular bar could merely comprise a highly polished wooden fixture with a mirror behind it and a tiled floor beneath," wrote Michael and Ariane Batterberry in *On the Town in New York*. "Now there were circular bars, revolving bars."

Women also worked in these upscale places, prompting one of the frequent patronizers of the clubs and speaks of the Roaring Twenties, poet/humorist Ogden Nash, to declare, "Barmaids are diviner than mermaids."

While women were downing drinks, the hemlines of their skirts were going up. The style was called flapper and the women who sported them, flappers. They danced to jazz, smoked cigarettes, "necked," went joyriding in fast cars with men toting their bootleg whiskey in pocket flasks, and got "blotto."

Across the country, this revolution in public behavior was likely to occur in a "honky-tonk." Instead of the band in the city speakeasy, it offered only a tinny piano. But the term *honky-tonk* was to persist long after *speakeasy* went into dictionaries as parlance of the past. Primarily because of romanticization in country–and–western music, *honky-tonk* came to mean a cheap saloon. It also was an unflattering adjective for a female who drank in such a spot. The "honky–tonk woman" was usually regarded as exactly the sort of woman that the prohibitionist/reformers such as Frances Willard had feared. One can only imagine her head bobbing in agreement, had she lived long enough, with sentiments expressed in a popular hit song composed by Tim Spencer, one of the founding members of the 1930s/40s country music group Sons of the Pioneers. It bemoaned the ruination of a man who had "a good wife" but lost her, in the words of the title, because of "Cigareets, Whusky, and Wild, Wild Women."

Myrna, Kate, Bette, Grace, and Faye

One may wonder, as well, what Frances Willard and her sister temperance campaigners would think if they could rise from their graves to learn that today a woman sipping brandy from a snifter between puffs on a cigar is as unremarkable as a man doing the same thing.

They might also inquire how such a calamity (in their view) could have happened. While changes in behavior may be attributed to what the anthropologists, historians, and sociologists like to call evolution, revolution, currents of history, and trends, the acceptance of women as drinkers owes a lot to the leadership of five exceptional stars of the silver screen.

Myrna Loy. Classy, smart, witty, both tough and tender, she not only kept up with William Powell in the *Thin Man* movies, but imbued a sense of elegance to a woman with a strong drink held delicately in hand during a long career as the epitome of the Hollywood "leading lady." She also gave a heartrending portrayal of a prosperous, suburban, alcoholic housewife as Paul Newman's mother in the movie version of John O'Hara's *From the Terrace.*

Katharine Hepburn. Whether she was Spencer Tracy's wife in *Adam's Rib* and *Guess Who's Coming to Dinner?* or the urbane socialite who almost married the wrong man in *The Philadelphia Story,* no woman could surpass Kate for independence of style in handling men and cocktails.

Betty Davis. All About Eve says it all.

Grace Kelly. In the Hepburn role in *High Society,* the remake of *The Philadelphia Story,* opposite Bing Crosby and Frank Sinatra, she knew her way around a martini as well as either of them. She also struggled to deal with Crosby as her on-screen alcoholic husband in *The Country Girl,* and matched Ray Milland and Robert Cummings in elegance in drinking in *Dial M for Murder.*

Faye Dunaway. There is no more sophisticated drinker than she in *Chinatown* and *Mommy Dearest,* nor truer hard-boiled honky-tonk woman than her Bonnie Parker in *Bonnie and Clyde.*

All of these admired and emulated stars said to the women who saw their films that it was not only acceptable for women to drink, but that they had as much right to do so as men.

Other Words on the Sexes and Spirits

Setting aside the admonition of George Herbert in *Jacula Prudentum* ("Where the drink goes in, there the wit goes out"), here is a sampling of what else has been said through the years about drinking by both sexes.

The poet Robert Graves seems to have caught the essence of the past and present relationship between men, women, drink, and tobacco when he wrote:

"Blonde or dark, sir?" says enough
Whether of women, drink, or snuff.

Fill all the glasses there, for why
Should every creature drink but I,
Why, man of morals, tell me why?
　　　　—Abraham Cowley, 1656

A very merry, dancing, drinking,
Laughing, quaffing, and unthinking time.
　　　　—John Dryden, 1700

Were I to prescribe a rule for drinking, it should be formed upon a saying quoted by Sir William Temple: the first glass for myself, the second for my friends, the third for good humor, and the fourth for mine enemies.
　　　　—Joseph Addison, *The Spectator,* 1711

We were to do more business after dinner; but after dinner is after dinner—an old saying and a true, "much drinking, little thinking."
　　　　—Jonathan Swift, 1712

One can drink too much, but one never drinks enough.
　　　　—Gotthold Ephraim Lessing, 1779

What's drinking?
A mere pause from thinking!
　　　　—George Noel Gordon, Lord Byron, 1824

Then stand to your glasses steady!
　　　　—Bartholemew Dowling, 1823–63

Candy
Is dandy
But liquor
Is quicker.
　　　　—Ogden Nash, 1931

I've made it a rule never to drink by daylight and never to refuse a drink after dark.
> —H. L. Mencken, 1945

I envy people who drink—at least they know what to blame everything on.
> —Oscar Levant

Drinking makes such fools of people, and people are such fools to begin with that it's compounding a felony.
> —Robert Benchley

Drink the first. Sip the second. Skip the third.
> —Knute Rockne

A soldier's a man;
A life's but a span;
Why, then, let a soldier drink.
> —Shakespeare, *Othello*

The only friends I have in this town are Haig and Haig.
> —John Barrymore

Alcohol removes warts. Not from me—from whomever I'm with.
> —Jackie Gleason

Boy was I drunk last night.
> —Mart Crowley, *The Boys in the Band*

16

WAS I IN HERE LAST NIGHT?

"A blonde drove me to drink, and my only regret is that I never thanked her."

—W. C. FIELDS

Although this book is a celebration of a happy association between human beings and "the water of life" in all its manifestations, it would be irresponsible for a book on spiritous drinks to ignore the reality that alcohol is not for everyone, and that for many its use frequently results in heartbreak and tragedy.

While there are studies indicating that moderate consumption of alcoholic beverages may have some health benefits, Dr. Charles Saul Lieber, professor of medicine and pathology at Mount Sinai School of Medicine in New York City, and director of the Bronx Veterans Administration alcohol programs, has warned, "No one ever knows who will develop a craving for alcohol and not be able to stop at that one drink."

Concerned about the toll of lives lost on highways as a result of drunken drivers and alarmed by the sharp rise in drinking by the young, various groups have carried out vigorous educational campaigns to emphasize their view that drinking to excess had become a major crisis.

One result of these campaigns was the end to the long–held view that someone who is "in his cups" is a subject of amusement. This was a reversal of a general attitude toward drunks on which a number of show–business careers were built and countless millions of people were amused for generations.

That attitude is exemplified in the movie *The Bank Dick,* in which W. C. Fields asked the question that is the title of this chapter. The bartender to whom it was posed was Shemp Howard, later a star in his own right as one of the Three Stooges.

"And," continues Fields, "did I spend a twenty–dollar bill?"

Howard replies, "Yes."

With a tug at his tie and a look of profound relief, Fields says, "Oh, boy! What a load that is off my mind. I thought I'd lost it."

No one in the history of drinking so embodied the likable drunk as Fields. Film critic Judith Crist in the introduction to the book *A Flask of Fields,* edited by Richard J. Anobile, saw him as "an American Falstaff at war with the twentieth century" and an "aged in the cask Gargantua trapped in middle–class morality, an alter ego for all of us in our daily frustrations."

He was indeed a very funny man who through hilarious scenes like the one in *The Bank Dick* left us a wealth of one–liners, bons mots, and jokes that have added greatly to the lore of drinking and the laughable inebriate.

Fields fostered that idea in one of his earliest sketches in vaudeville, titled "The Drunkard." Alas, that's what he was offscreen. Unrestrained and irresponsible drinking was the cause of his death on Christmas Day, 1946, at a time in America when everyone found humor in the figure of the drunken fellow (though never in a besotted woman).

The heavy-drinking character played by Phil Harris kept the radio and television audiences of Jack Benny's shows laughing for years, as did comedic actor Billy De Wolfe and a Hollywood character actor of the thirties and forties, Jack Norton, who built a career on portraying a tuxedo-clad falling-down drunk.

A booze-loving, happy singer was the stage persona of Dean Martin. A golfer, he once quipped, "If you drink, don't drive. Don't even putt."

Television funny man Jackie Gleason did his monologues with a real drink in his hand. After sipping it, he rolled his eyes and tossed back his head to a drumroll, then bellowed, "How sweet it is!" Playing opposite his affable Joe the Bartender was a happy drunk, Crazy Guggenham. Played by rubber-faced Frank Fontaine with a battered and out-of-shape fedora, he continued the stereotype of the alcoholic. Gleason also created the constantly drunk Reggie Van Gleason to the amusement of television viewers who at the time found nothing in someone being soused that wasn't funny.

Nor did audiences of the 1970s find anything but hilarity from portrayals of lovable drunks by Foster Brooks, the town drunk Otis Campbell of Andy Griffith's fictional Mayberry, or Jim Baccus as the boozy millionaire of *Gilligan's Island*.

While television, movies, and radio fostered inebriation as a means of getting laughs, they did not invent the amusing drunk. Shakespeare did it in the form of Sir John Falstaff, centuries before Judith Crist found him reincarnated as W. C. Fields. In the language of the Bard of Avon, dictionaries list more phrases for the state of inebriation than synonyms for any other word, with new ones constantly coming into use. Benjamin Franklin had a list of 228. Two centuries later, *The Dictionary of American Slang* contained nearly 400. They begin with *alcoholic* and run the gamut of the alphabet to *wino* and *zapped*.

In addressing the terminology of drinking in reference to himself, Jackie Gleason could not resist joking, "I'm no alcoholic, I'm a drunkard. There's a difference. A drunkard doesn't go to meetings."

Other celebrities also owned up to their serious problems with drinking. One of the finest of Britain's actors, Michael Caine, said, "The best research for playing a drunk is being a British actor for twenty years." His countryman Peter Lawford joked that at the height of his bouts with the bottle, "I was spilling more than Dean Martin drank." Welsh-born

Anthony Hopkins attributed his heavy drinking to insecurity about his acting ability. "It was madness," he said in retrospect, because drinking too much interfered with his acting. "I was just a drunken bore."

Although Spencer Tracy's admiring fans had no idea that he was a drunk, he was infamous among Hollywood insiders for his binges. "Hell, I used to take two-week lunch hours," he said. "Anyone who stayed drunk for twenty-five years as I did would have to be in trouble."

Perhaps because the motion-picture industry had been made aware of the problem of alcoholism in Hollywood, it dealt with the phenomenon in a number of remarkable films.

First to tackle the subject in 1937 was *A Star Is Born*. It starred Janet Gaynor as Esther Blodgett, known to her movie fans as Vicky Lester. She was the adoring wife of alcoholic movie actor Norman Maine (Fredric March). The film was remade in 1954 with plenty of songs for Judy Garland as the suffering spouse of James Mason. Remade again in 1976, it had a rock-and-roll sound track and starred Barbra Streisand and Kris Kristofferson.

Relentlessly stark in depicting the tortured life of an alcoholic, brilliantly and grimly played by Ray Milland, was *The Lost Weekend*, in 1945.

For 1954's *The Country Girl*, Grace Kelly won an Oscar as Best Actress as the wife of Bing Crosby, an alcoholic singer trying to make a comeback.

In *Days of Wine and Roses*, 1962, Jack Lemmon delivered a performance as an alcoholic that was the polar opposite of his happy Ensign Pulver pushing pseudo scotch on the unsuspecting Navy nurse in *Mr. Roberts*.

It was hoped that such films might have an impact on those who realized as they watched them that they were seeing themselves on the screen. According to Kris Kristofferson, that is what happened to him. He told an interviewer that at a time when he was sober he had seen himself on a television program and in *A Star Is Born* at the same time. "I realized it was my own life I was seeing on the screen," he said. "A rock-and-roll star ruining himself drinking. I'll never touch it again, because I saw myself being lowered into my own coffin."

But alcoholism has not been the bane of only Hollywood. Some of the world's greatest writers were either ruined by it or died as a result. The composer of some of America's most beloved and enduring songs, Stephen Foster, literally killed himself falling down drunk. The British poet Lionel Johnson was killed when he tumbled off a barstool. Prob-

The grim life of an alcoholic was brilliantly portrayed by Ray Milland in Lost Weekend.
Bettman Archives

ably the most popular authors to die from a lifetime of drinking were Edgar Allan Poe, Jack London, Stephen Crane, Sinclair Lewis, Ambrose Bierce, Eugene O'Neill, F. Scott Fitzgerald, and Welsh poet Dylan Thomas.

In the world of sports, arguably the most famous and beloved player to succomb to accumulated results of alcohol abuse was Mickey Mantle.

Robert Young, whose acting success reached its zenith in television's *Father Knows Best* and as Dr. Marcus Welby, said, "I've been sick all my life with fear of some imagined disaster that never did eventuate. When I became an actor I constantly felt I wasn't worthy, that I had no right to be a star. Naturally, I tried to find a way out. Alcoholism was the inevitable result."

Was it? Is it true that for some people alcoholism must be the inevitable outcome of taking the first drink? The question of why the famous and the nonfamous drink to excess is not going to be answered here, but it is to be hoped that scientific research, perhaps in the burgeoning field of genetics, as well as sociological studies, will one day produce the answer.

By law, labels on liquor bottles must carry warnings of the risks to some categories of people in consuming spirits.

Hats are raised as Prohibition laws are lifted.
Bettman Archives

There is no question that some individuals should not drink at all: women who are pregnant or are trying to conceive, anyone taking prescription or over-the-counter medicine, hypoglycemics, anyone known to have an addictive nature, and drivers.

While there is no likelihood that the mistake of Prohibition is going to be repeated in the United States, activists in the effort to alert the public to the consequences of alcohol abuse found a new cause for alarm in 1996 when a leading maker of alcoholic beverages decided to break a traditional policy of the liquor industry by advertising its products on radio and television.

Advertising

Although advertising of liquor has never been prohibited by law in the United States, distillers were acutely aware that the consumers of their products brought to the experience a potential for abuse. Consequently, liquor manufacturers in the form of the Distilled Spirits Council of the United States voluntarily banned advertising liquors on radio in 1936 and on television in 1948.

But in 1996 Seagram announced that because of lagging sales, it intended to resume the advertising on television on a limited test basis in Corpus Christi, Texas. The 30-second commercials were to run for one month for Crown Royal whiskey, and the policy was later extended to other parts of the country.

Arthur Shapiro, Seagram executive vice president of marketing and strategy, in announcing the plan said, "We believe that distilled spirits should be able to access advertising in a responsible way on television and radio in the same manner as beer and wine."

The spirits council also pointed out that the blurring of lines between print, broadcast, and cable and communications made less of a distinction between the types of advertising.

This reasoning notwithstanding, the Seagram plan was met with immediate resistance. Declared George Hacker of the Washington–based Center for Science in the Public Interest, "Seagram's decision to start running television ads is a cynical, profiteering attempt to exploit a new generation of young people by attracting them to drink hard liquor." The group also coordinated publication in the *New York Times* of a full-page open letter to Seagram Chief Operating Officer Edgar Bronfman Jr. It protested against the company's plan and solicited readers to call Bronfman at the firm's New York offices—the number was in the ad—to register their objections.

Cascade whiskey advertisements claimed a medical seal of approval.
Courtesy United Distillers Archive, Schenley Collection, George A. Dickel files

Government also enlisted in the ranks of opponents. Massachusetts Democratic Representative Joseph Kennedy announced his intention to introduce a bill in Congress to make the advertising ban a matter of federal law, similar to the banning of cigarette advertising. President Clinton issued a statement calling the ban on ads for hard liquor "a good thing and has helped protect children."

The issue seemed destined for resolution only in the federal courts, where the arguments against advertising liquor on the air would be weighed against the constitutional rights of liquor makers to free speech and expression.

Yet no liquor advertising in any form had ever openly made an appeal to children in hopes of making them drinkers when they reached adulthood. The basic purpose of advertising whiskey and other spirits has always been to emphasize brand identity and consumer loyalty simply by portraying the product. The intention was—and is—to encourage a drinker not to simply ask a bartender for "a scotch and soda" but "a Dewar's and soda," for example.

None of the examples of advertising past and present studied for the purpose of writing this book could in any way be interpreted as recruiting children or laying the foundation for their future enlistment in the ranks of drinkers. That has been a hallmark of the creators of the mass media of entertainment: See the movie *Saturday Night Fever,* the *Porky's* film series, any movie set on a contemporary college campus, etc.

Drinking "the hard stuff" as a rite of passage also has been a favorite theme in literature. An underage person in America has been far less likely to be tempted to try drinking from a liquor ad than after a reading of Amory Blaine in F. Scott Fitzgerald's *This Side of Paradise,* and J. D. Salinger's *Catcher in the Rye* or William Goldman's first novel of youth, *The Temple of Gold.*

In the latter, a pair of high school boys, having nothing to do on a spring night in a small town, and neither knowing "for beans about alcohol," raid a liquor cabinet. One guzzles rum, the other scotch. Quickly drunk, the one who chose the rum says he is in his cups and then asks his partner, "Isn't that the stupidest expression?"

Caught staggering in the street, they are hauled to jail by a cop, an event that the novel's narrator proudly boasts, "made my reputation" as school clown. Not revealed by the narrator was how getting drunk the first time left him feeling the day after.

The Hangover

The aftereffects of too much drinking—and remedies for it—were set down by humorist Robert Benchley in his essay "Coffee Versus Gin."

He wrote: "This 'old wives'' superstition that a cup of black coffee will 'put you back on your feet' with a hangover is either propaganda by the coffee people or the work of dilettante drinkers who get giddy on cooking sherry. A man with a *real* hangover is in no mood to be told 'Just take a cup of black coffee' or 'The thing for you is a couple of aspirin.' A real hangover is nothing to try out family remedies on. The only cure for a real hangover is death."

Had Benchley been around in 1884, he would have referred to a remedy for the headaches and muscle pains as a "brain duster." At a time when absinthe was still legally available, a chilled "pick-me-up" was likely to have it as the chief ingredient. For a less acute case of "morning-after," a remedy was equal quantities of beer, porter, champagne, and ginger ale, known as a Blue Velvet.

Current recommendations for a preventing/curing of the hangover include:

1. Water! Drink it before bedtime and keep it handy. Alcohol is a diuretic, and drying out is a major factor of the agony. Coffee is also a diuretic, so slurping up lots of it will only exacerbate the problem. Mineral water is good for reducing acid in the stomach. Antacids are also recommended. So is chicken soup (replaces fluid).

2. Milk! A glass before you even start drinking will slow alcohol absorption.

3. Stay away from pot-still spirits (malt whiskey and brandy). A continuous-still (patent) removes more impurities and toxins.

4. Vitamins B and C detoxify the liver.

5. Fructose. Helps burn off the alcohol and replaces blood sugar. So does alcohol, but taking "the hair of the dog that bit you" will put you on the slippery slope that leads to another hangover. Bread is a good source of fructose.

6. Sleep it off, if you're able to.

Of course, the way to avoid a hangover is to take it easy drinking the night before the day after. Aristotle, who never had a drink of distilled liquor in his life, nonetheless came up with the best preventative of hangovers (and all other possible human troubles): "Be moderate in all things."

If you think that being hung over will affect your work, one researcher into the question found no cause for alarm. Siegfried Streufert at Pennsylvania State University studied managers and professionals who had consumed four to six drinks the night before. He reported, "These people did feel miserable. Yet their decision-making performance was not affected."

Remembrances of Things Past

Hangovers notwithstanding, many of today's actions, having been sorted and sifted by our brains into memories, turn out to be things we choose to do again. Objects we once possessed but discarded suddenly are longed for once more, only to be found in antique shops or flea markets at outrageous prices.

This phenomenon also pertains to the experience of spirited drinks. Like old toys, radios, television sets, clothing, furniture, and all the other relics of our past, the ephemera and artifacts of the history of distilled drinks have become collectibles. Like cigar bands, bottle labels have found a niche in the world of collecting. So are the palm–sized, one–shot individual bottles sold on airplanes and in liquor stores.

Old bottles are also prized. The most likely places to find old liquor bottles are flea markets, garage sales, and antique stores. Some distilleries, such as Jack Daniel's, put out special commemorative bottlings in limited numbers that are guaranteed never to be produced again.

Although the author is not a bottle collector, I do have one that I cherish. An emptied seven–ounce, glass, cork–stoppered, gracefully tapered, "Warranted" pocket flask, it was found by my brother–in–law, William Detwiler, while he was making repairs to the house built by my Irish grandfather and a few of his friends a hundred years ago. It was tucked away in a corner of the front porch roof.

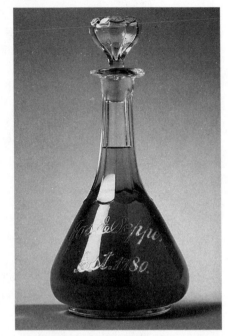

Among old bottle collectibles, a James E. Pepper bar decanter, circa 1910.

Courtesy United Distillers Archive, Schenley Collection, James E. Pepper files

Delighted and amused to have it, all of us in the Jeffers-Detwiler families assumed it had been set down by my grandfather or a helper, forgotten about, and sealed up. But as a consequence of my research for this book I learned we were mistaken. It was the tradition of Irish builders to conceal somewhere in houses and other buildings an empty whiskey bottle as a blessing.

Judging by how well the old house has withstood the storms of nature and a century of everyday living, and how nicely those who were born in it and then moved out of it and into houses of their own have turned out, it worked.

This book began with a few words on the world's oldest means of quenching thirst. It is fitting, therefore, to conclude the book by returning to that subject. Accordingly, here is a favorite recitation of Senator Alan K. Simpson of Wyoming. He has maintained that it was originally spoken by an inebriated politician who had mistakenly stumbled into a meeting of the local Women's Temperance Union, only to be invited to speak by the chairwoman in the expectation that the man would become an example to be cited by the teetotaler ladies in waging their campaign to drive John Barleycorn from the nation. As related by Senator Simpson and recorded by the author of this book from the C-SPAN telecast of his remarks, what the dragooned speaker offered the temperance ladies was this:

THE TOAST TO WATER

I have seen it glisten in tiny teardrops on the face of infancy. I have seen it go coursing down the dimpled cheeks of youth. And I have seen it in rushing torrents down the wrinkled cheeks of age. I have seen it in the blades of grass and leaves of trees, sparkling like tiny diamonds as the morning sun rose in resplendent glory over the eastern hills. I have seen it in the heavens as they shudder and weep in gentle rain and splash in shimmering droplets upon the warm and fertile earth to nurture the tiny tendrils of fruit and grain. I have seen it come tumbling down the mountainside in cascades fleecy as a bridal veil with the music of liquid silver filling the vast forest arches with symphonies. And I have seen it in silent rivers rippling over pebbly bottoms and roaring in mad cataracts over precipitous waterfalls in its rush to join the Father of Waters. And I have seen it in the Father of Waters going in majestic sweep to join the ocean. I have seen it in the ocean on whose broad bosom float the battleships of the nations and the commerce of the world. But ladies, as a beverage it's a damn failure!

Glossary

Absinthe	A licorice–flavored product of wormwood, illegal since 1912 in the United States because of its damaging effects on the mind.
Advocaat	Dutch liqueur similar in flavor to eggnog.
Aging	Maturation of distilled spirits in casks, usually made of oak.
Amaretto	Italian liqueur based on apricots.
Amer Picon	French bitters.
Angostura Bitters	Rum–based product of Trinidad.
Anise	A plant of the carrot family whose fragrant seeds (aniseed) are similar in flavor to absinthe.
Anisette	Licorice-flavored French liqueur.
Aperitif	Before–dinner appetite stimulant.
Aquavit	Scandinavian drink similar to vodka.
Aquavite	Italian spelling of the Latin *aqua vitae*, meaning "water of life"; in Gaelic, *uisge beatha*, which became whiskey.
Armagnac	French brandy.
Benedictine	French liqueur.
Bitters	Neutral spirits flavored with botanicals.
Blended	A mixture of several whiskeys.
Bourbon	Kentucky whiskey, made from a mash of at least 51 percent corn.
Branch	Plain water.
Brandy	Distillation of grapes. Fruit brandies are made from various fruits.
Calvados	Apple brandy made in the Normandy region of France.
Campari	Red Italian aperitif, similar to bitters.
Canadian	Grain-based whiskey made in Canada.

Charring	Burning the interiors of oak casks to charcoalize the walls of the bar-rels.
Chartreuse	French herbal liqueur made by Carthusian monks.
Chaser	A mild drink, such as water or beer, taken after a spiritous drink.
Cider	Pressed juice of apples. Hard cider is fermented.
Cinzano	Brand of Italian vermouth.
Cocktail	A chilled alcoholic beverage made with at least one mixer.
Cognac	Brandy produced in the Cognac region of France.
Cointreau	Clear, orange-flavored liqueur.
Collins	Iced tall drink made with various liquors, mixed with citrus juice and sugar and topped with club soda.
Cordial	A liqueur.
Diastase	Sugar-producing enzyme resulting from fermentation of grain that is dried, added to water, and then distilled to produce alcohol.
Distillation	Evaporation and precipitation of alcohol in the boiling of a mixture (mash) of grain and water.
Doubling	A second distillation of spirits to improve both strength and flavor.
Drambuie	Scotch-based liqueur.
Feints	Product yielded in third stage in whiskey distillation.
Fermentation	Conversion of grain starches to sugars.
Finish	The aftertaste of an alcoholic beverage.
Foreshot	Product yielded in the first stage of whiskey distillation.
Gin	Distilled fermented grains flavored with juniper.
Grain alcohol	Nearly pure alcohol.
Grand Marnier	Cognac-based, orange-flavored French liqueur.

Grappa	Strong brandy made from pulpy remnants of the wine-making process.
Highball	An iced tall drink made with liquor and water, club soda, or other mixer.
Highlands	Scotch-making region of northern Scotland.
High wines	The final output of the second distillation in the whiskey-making process; distillate ready to be aged.
Irish whiskey	A blend of distilled grains made in Ireland.
Liqueur	After-dinner alcoholic drink with strong fruit, berry, or other flavors added.
Lowball	A drink served on the rocks in an old-fashioned glass.
Low wines	First yield of the pot-still distilling method.
Malt	Grain softened to germination by soaking in water.
Mash	Grain steeped in hot water to produce fermentation.
Neat	Unmixed, non-iced liquor in a shot glass.
On-the-rocks	A drink with ice cubes.
Ouzo	Aniseed-based clear Greek liquor that turns milky when mixed with water or ice.
Patent still	Cooking apparatus that distills spirits continuously. Also known as a Coffey still.
Pot still	Onion-shaped, copper-lined cooker used in the distillation of liquors.
Proof	Strength of alcoholic contents.
Rock & Rye	Citrus liqueur made by steeping fruit in rye whiskey and sweetening with rock candy.
Rum	Distillate of sugarcane or molasses.
Rye	American grain whiskey.

Saccharification	Conversion of grain starch to sugar by the diastase enzyme.
Sambuca	Italian anise–flavored liqueur.
Scotch	The whiskey of Scotland, distilled from fermented grain to make single-malts and blends.
Sour mash	Also known as "backset." A portion of the liquid strained from the first distillation that is added to the next distillation.
Tennessee	Whiskey that is flavored by filtration through a minimum of ten feet of sugar–maple charcoal.
Tequila	The national alcoholic drink of Mexico, taken straight and followed with a taste of salt and lemon or lime.
Triple sec	Clear, orange–flavored liqueur.
Vermouth	Italian or French herbal wine fortified with brandy, a component of the martini.
Vodka	Clear, unaged, grain distillate; traditional beverage of Eastern Europe.
Wheated bourbon	A bourbon made of wheat instead of rye grain.
Whiskey	Distilled fermented grains. (Also spelled whisky.)

Sources

"I have taken more out of alcohol than it has taken out of me."

—WINSTON CHURCHILL

There may be times when it's better to do something alone, including drinking, but writing a book on drinking could not be a solitary undertaking. So here's a toast of gratitude for the aid provided by my friend and computer wizard who went where no man had ever gone before to explore the vast reaches of cyberspace in order to ferret out every bit and byte of data in the universe of spiritous drink—Al Leibholz.

For anecdotal material related to the reasons behind their personal preferences in beverages I am grateful to Sid Goldstein (a straight-up martini, Jack Daniel's, and Wild Turkey man), Mike Ludlum (Armagnac, cognac, and other brandies), Kevin Gordon (the spirits of Spain), my seagoing nephew Michael P. Jeffers (tequila and sambuca), Gene Valentino (bourbon), and Peter Cane (scotch).

My thanks for assistance in obtaining facts, photographs, and other illustrative materials go to Jeff Potash of Schieffelin and Somerset regarding scotch. A treasure trove of material on American whiskeys was provided by Mike Veach of United Distillers for W. L. Weller, Old Fitzgerald, Old Charter, I. W. Harper, George Dickel, and the Canadian brands Schenley, Gibson, MacNaugton, and O.F.C.; Chris McCurry of the Ancient Age Distillery; Lisa Appleby of Jim Beam; Keith Steer of the Heaven Hill Distillery; Sheila Swerling of Four Roses; Rachel Denliker of Wild Turkey; and Bill Samuels Jr., the president of Maker's Mark. Curtis Field, librarian, consul general of Canada, assisted me on the Canadian distilling industry. Christopher P. McCrory, brand manager for Sazerac, provided material concerning Ancient Age Distilling and single-barrel bourbon. Patricia Henry of Jack Daniel's Distillery furnished material on Tennessee whiskey in general and Jack Daniel's in particular, as well as the other products of the Brown-Forman Corporation (Southern Comfort, Canadian Mist) and the firm's American representation of foreign distillers, including Bushmills, Usher's, and Glenmorangie scotch, Pepe Lopez Tequila, Oblio Sambucas, and Korbel California brandy. And Eily Kilgannon, Irish Distillers Limited.

Should you wish to seek even more information, here are addresses that may prove useful:

SCOTCH

The Classic Malt Society
2 Park Avenue, 17th Floor
New York, New York 10016

IRISH

The Brown–Forman Corporation
Bushmills Irish Whiskies
PO Box 1080
Louisville, Kentucky 40201–1080

Midleton Distillery
Midleton County
Cork, Ireland

BOURBON

The Ancient Age Distillery
1001 Wilkinson Boulevard
Frankfort, Kentucky 40601

Bartons Brands, Ltd.
The Barton Distillery
1 Barton Road
Bardstown, Kentucky 40004

The Bernheim Distillery
1701 West Breckinridge
PO Box 740010
Louisville, Kentucky 40210–7410

The Early Times Distillery
The Brown–Forman Corporation
850 Dixie Highway
PO Box 1080
Louisville, Kentucky 40201

The Four Roses Distillery
1224 Bonds Hill Road
Lawrenceburg, Kentucky 40342

The Heaven Hill Distillery
Highway 49, Loretto Road
PO Box 729
Bardstown, Kentucky 40004–0729

The Jim Beam Distilleries
Clermont, Kentucky 40110

Maker's Mark Bourbon
Loretto, Kentucky 40037

The Wild Turkey Distillery
Highway 1510, Box 180
Lawrenceburg, Kentucky 40342

TENNESSEE

George A. Dickel's Cascade Distillery
1950 Cascade Hollow Road
PO Box 490
Tullahoma, Tennessee 37388

The Jack Daniel Distillery
Highway #55
PO Box 199
Lynchburg, Tennessee 37352

CANADIAN

Canadian Mist Whiskey
The Brown–Forman Corporation
PO Box 1080
Louisville, Kentucky 40201–1080

Joseph Seagram & Sons Inc.
375 Park Avenue
New York, New York 10152

TEQUILA, SAMBUCA, CALIFORNIA BRANDIES

The Brown-Forman Corporation

AMERICAN DISTILLERIES WITH TOURS

(Call for details)

The Ancient Age Distillery
The Leestown Company, Inc.
1001 Wilkinson Boulevard
Frankfort, Kentucky 40601
Phone: (502) 223-7641

George A. Dickel's Cascade Distillery
1950 Cascade Hollow Road
PO Box 490
Tullahoma, Tennessee 37388
Phone: (615) 857-3124

The Heaven Hill Distillery
Highway 49, Loretto Road
PO Box 729
Bardstown, Kentucky 40004-0729
Phone: (502) 348-3921

The Jack Daniel Distillery
Highway 55
PO Box 199
Lynchburg, Tennessee 37352
Phone: (615) 759-4221

Maker's Mark Bourbon
Loretto, Kentucky 40037
Phone: (502) 865-2099

The Wild Turkey Distillery
Highway 1510, Box 180
Lawrenceburg, Kentucky 40342

MUSEUM

Jim Beam Companies operate Jim Beam's American Outpost, which includes a barrel-making (cooperage) museum and a decanter museum. It also has a rackhouse (warehouse) and "the oldest still in America" on display. A craft shop offers Kentucky handicrafts and "a wide variety of Jim Beam novelties." It is reached by car by taking Exit 112 (Bardstown/Bernheim Forest) to Highway 245. Turn east 1½ miles. Phone: (502) 543-9877.

LITERATURE

Malt Advocate. This quarterly magazine promises "to be the most informative and entertaining drinks-and-lifestyle publication by promoting the intelligent, responsible, and joyful consumption of the world's finer beers and whiskeys." At newsstands and by subscription ($12.95 a year).

Malt Advocate
3416 Oak Hill Rd.
Emmaus, PA 18049
Phone: (800) 610-MALT
E-Mail: maltman 999@aol.com
Internet:
http://maltadvocate.com/maltadvocate

Single Malt Connoisseur's Club. Primarily a retailer offering discounts on single-malt scotch to members, the firm also has a wide range of books and booklets on spiritous drinks.

Single Malt Connoisseur's Club
200 Fillmore Street
San Francisco, CA 94115
Phone: (800) 637-0292
Fax: (415) 346-1812

NEWSLETTERS

The Kentucky Bourbon Circle
PO Box 1
Clermont, Kentucky 40110-9980
(Free)

Single-Barrel Bourbon Society
PO Box 1031
Louisville, Kentucky 40201
(Free)

The Bourbon County Reader
3712 North Broadway
Box 298
Chicago, Illinois 60613
(Send stamped return envelope for sample and cost)

F. Paul Pacult's Spirit Journal
421-13 Route 59
Monsey, New York 10952
($49 per year)

FURTHER READING

Batterberry, Michael and Ariane. *On the Town in New York.* Harper & Row, New York: 1973.

Blue, Anthony Dias. *The Complete Book of Mixed Drinks.* Harper Perennial, New York: 1993.

Brander, Michael. *Brander's Guide to Scotch Whiskey.* Lyons & Burford, Publishers, New York: 1996.

———. *The Original Scotch.* Hutchinson, London: 1974.

Conrad III, Barnaby. *The Martini.* Chronicle Books, San Francisco: 1995.

Faith, Nicholas. *The Simon & Schuster Pocket Guide to Cognac and Other Brandies.* Simon & Schuster, New York: 1987.

Feller, Robyn M. *The Complete Bartender.* Berkley Books, New York: 1990.

Greenberg, Emannuel and Madeline. *The Pocket Guide to Spirits and Liqueurs.* Perigee Books, the Putnam Publishing Group, New York: 1983.

Jackson, Michael. *Bar & Cocktail Companion.* Running Press, Philadelphia: 1995.

———. *Complete Guide to Single Malt Scotch.* Running Press, Philadelphia: 1989.

Lamond, John, and Robin Tucek. *The Malt Whisky File.* The Wine Appreciation Guild, San Francisco: 1995.

MacLean, Charles. *The Mitchell Beazley Pocket Whisky Book*. Reed Consumer Books Limited, London: 1993.

McDowall, R. J. S. *The Whiskies of Scotland*. Abelard Schuman, New York: 1967.

Moss, Michael S., and John R. Hume. *The Making of Scotch Whisky*. James & James, Edinburgh: 1981.

Mr. Boston Deluxe Official Bartenders' Guide. Warner Books, New York: 1981.

The New International Bartender's Guide. Random House, New York: 1984.

Poister, John J. *The New American Bartender's Guide*. Penguin Books, New York: 1989.

Regan, Gary, and Mardee Haidin Regan. *The Book of Bourbon and Other Fine American Whiskies*. Chapters Publishing Ltd., Shelburne, Vermont: 1995.

Index